Liturgical Snapshots

Liturgical Snapshots

Reflections on the Richness of
Our Worship Tradition

Owen F. Cummings

Paulist Press
New York / Mahwah, NJ

The scripture quotations contained herein are from the New Revised Standard Version: Catholic Edition Copyright © 1989 and 1993, by the Division of Christian Education of the National Council of the Churches of Christ in the United States of America. Used by permission. All rights reserved.

Excerpts from the English translation of *The Roman Missal* © 2010, International Commission on English in the Liturgy Corporation. All rights reserved.

Excerpt from Dylan Thomas, "Do Not Go Gentle into That Good Night," from Sandra M. Gilbert, ed., *Inventions of Farewell: A Book of Elegies.* New York and London: Norton, 2001.

Cover image courtesy of Shutterstock.com/Lindsay Douglas
Cover design by Sharyn Banks
Book design by Lynn Else

Library of Congress Cataloging-in-Publication Data

Cummings, Owen F.
    Liturgical snapshots : reflections on the richness of our worship tradition / Owen F. Cummings.
        p. cm.
    Includes bibliographical references (p.   ).
    ISBN 978-0-8091-4783-0 (alk. paper) — ISBN 978-1-61643-671-1 1. Catholic Church—Liturgy—History. I. Title.
    BX1975.C86 2012
    264'.02—dc23

                                                                    2012020496

Published by Paulist Press
997 Macarthur Boulevard
Mahwah, New Jersey 07430

www.paulistpress.com

Printed and bound in the
United States of America

Contents

Dedicated to Archbishop John G. Vlazny,
archbishop of Portland in Oregon,
and Monsignor J. Richard Paperini,
president-rector of Mount Angel Seminary

Introduction

A common complaint among those who taught liturgical and sacramental theology in the 1970s was the real dearth of suitable textbooks in these areas. The revised liturgical rites flowing from Vatican II were gradually implemented, but it seems to me that theology did not keep pace immediately with the liturgical renewal. Today, however, by way of contrast, many fine introductions to liturgical theology and to the sacraments are available to the interested reader, and I have benefited from them. This little book is not an introduction to liturgical or sacramental theology, nor is it a "video" laying out a panoramic and sequential liturgical-sacramental perspective. Rather, it is a series of reflections, or "snapshots," around liturgy and sacraments.

Probably all of us have oodles of snapshots in our homes, perhaps neatly and chronologically arranged in photograph albums or gathered in many different boxes and envelopes. A linear photographic album displaying year by year the course of a person's life has its own unique charm and attraction. One can observe the growth, development, and change that have occurred over the years. That is most valuable. Opening a box of photographs and looking through some individual snapshots can be equally valuable. The limited view and perspective that come from individual snapshots may perhaps better assist and promote an understanding of the subject photographed. Individual snapshots may draw my attention to aspects of the subject that may become glossed over in a linear view. Thus, the liturgical-sacramental snapshots in this little volume will, it is hoped, draw the reader's attention to various aspects of the whole liturgical-sacramental continuum.

My point of departure comes to expression in three quotations. The first is from Vatican II's Constitution on the Sacred

Liturgy: "Mother Church earnestly desires that all the faithful should be led to that full, conscious and active participation in liturgical celebrations which is demanded by the very nature of the liturgy" (par. 14). In the year 2012 that statement will have been fifty years old, and if we accept Blessed John Henry Newman's idea that it takes a century to receive a council, then we may be halfway toward the experience of that full, conscious, and active participation in the liturgy. So, we just have another fifty years (or the other halfway!) to go for the full implementation of the council!

That takes me readily to my second quotation, this time from Pope Benedict XVI. In his encyclical *Sacramentum Caritatis* he writes, "The difficulties and even the occasional abuses which were noted…cannot overshadow the benefits and the validity of the liturgical renewal, whose riches are yet to be fully explored" (par. 3). While acknowledging difficulties, the Holy Father also emphasizes the benefits of the liturgical renewal consequent upon the council as well as a depth of riches yet to be mined.

The third quotation comes from Msgr. Kevin Irwin, professor of liturgy at the Catholic University of America. He has wisely observed, "Liturgical reforms are comparatively easy to accomplish. Church renewal takes a lifetime."[1] What Msgr. Irwin is writing about is entirely obvious: the renewal of the church and, moreover, the renewal of the church through the liturgy. What is left unsaid but is implied is that the renewal of the church is about you and me. If we are not renewed and renewed through the liturgy, then, quite bluntly, church renewal does not happen, or at the very least it is diminished. A lifetime of daily and weekly effort is required. It is hoped that this little book will speak to the perspective of these three quotations concerning the liturgy.

How will it do so? The book begins with a chapter on the Blessed Trinity in the liturgy. Both the liturgical year and the celebration of the Eucharist have a strong trinitarian shape. The liturgy is about God, who is Trinity, divinizing us. As beautifully put by the late Aidan Kavanagh, OSB, the liturgy is "our summons to a community of Three Persons who remain present to, for, and with us at every step along the way."[2] Always and everywhere the Triune God is inviting humankind to communion with himself, and par excellence in-the-liturgy-in-the-church. We are opened up to this divinizing perspective in the first chapter. The second chapter describes worship and the Catholic imagination or, as David Tracy would have it, the analogical imagination. The God present to us everywhere and always becomes intensely present to us in the actual building that is the church and in and through its liturgical furniture and arrangement. This is the Catholic imagination at work.

No Catholic liturgical rite is celebrated without the holy scriptures, and it is to the scriptures that the third chapter is devoted. Through the insights and poetry of the late sixteenth- and early seventeenth-century priest-poet George Herbert, we attempt to recognize the dynamism of God's word, a word that mediates Christ's presence. That word is preached about especially in Sunday celebrations of the Eucharist. Preaching is a challenging activity, and in chapter 4 we look to some masters of the preached word, past and present, to help us plumb the meaning of preaching.

The center of all liturgy for Catholics is, of course, the Eucharist. Five chapters are devoted to the Eucharist, beginning with the trinitarian emphasis of chapter 5, which confirms and reinforces the perspective of chapter 1. Long before Vatican II, in the early part of the twentieth century, the Buckfast Benedictine Anscar Vonier developed an understanding of the Eucharist that in some ways anticipated the horizons of that council. His insights constitute chapter 6. Chapter 7 tries to demonstrate that as the Eucharist divinizes us, so also its ritual performance may humanize us. It does this by having us rehearse in ritual form all the constitutive elements of what it means to be a human being: assembly, listening and speaking, eating and drinking, and dismissal. These human experiences correlate with the liturgical experiences of the Eucharist.

One of the most difficult and challenging aspects of what it is to be a human person has to do with the experience of suffering. This is tackled in an initial and inchoate way in chapter 8, using especially the insights of the historian Margaret Spufford.

We see her writing reflecting a very difficult life, with no evasion of the hard questions suffering poses for the Christian believer. At the same time we see in her living in, through, and with the Eucharist what we might call a performative theodicy.

Chapter 9 takes up the theology of Benediction. Benediction may not be celebrated as frequently as it once was, but it offers a privileged moment to reflect further on eucharistic meaning and significance. Insight is afforded here especially by the reflection of the Anglican systematic theologian John Macquarrie.

In chapter 10 we turn to the practice of reconciliation, trying to tap into the human experience and theological meaning of the sacrament of penance and reconciliation. That theological meaning is approached obliquely through novels and poetry. Arguably good novels and pleasing poetry continue to hold our attention both by expanding our understanding of the complexities of life and by inviting us to a deeper sense of personal identity in an ambiguous world. All earthly human life comes to an end in death, and when it comes to this reality, prosaic theology seldom is helpful. Far more helpful, as with the last chapter on reconciliation, is the medium of poetry. In chapter 11 John Henry Newman's epic poem "The Dream of Gerontius" is engaged as a way of retrieving a deeper Christian understanding of death, judgment, and purgatory. Finally, chapter 12 sets out some thoughts on the prayer of petition and intercession. Throughout the liturgy we petition God and we pray for others. This chapter invites us to think more philosophically about the meaning of petition and intercession.

Liturgical Snapshots ultimately has but one purpose: to help us move into closer communion with our Triune God through a deeper awareness of various aspects of the liturgy. If it promotes this purpose in some small measure, the author will be well pleased.

The author is well pleased indeed to acknowledge with great gratitude the support, insight, and editorial acumen of Dr. Nancy de Flon, church historian and editor at Paulist Press. Without her skill these little snapshots would never have been developed!

1

The Liturgical Trinity: Mystery of Love

The notion that Christian theology is to be seen as concerned with the mystery of God, the trinitarian God who loved us in Christ and calls us to participate in the mystery which he is, suggests to me that the main concern of theology is not so much to elucidate anything, as to prevent us, the Church, from dissolving the mystery that lies at the heart of the faith—dissolving it, or missing it altogether, by failing truly to engage with it....The heart of the matter is sharing in the mystery of love which God is....

Andrew Louth[1]

These words from the Orthodox theologian Andrew Louth are right on the mark: "The heart of the matter is sharing in the mystery of love which God is." This is the Trinity. In the early 1970s I was taught the doctrine of the Trinity in a semester-long course based on the codex authored by the Canadian Jesuit Fr. Frederick E. Crowe. This codex was itself constructed around the two-volume work, *De Deo Trino*, of Crowe's friend and colleague, Fr. Bernard Lonergan, SJ. It was a marvelous course, helped us to see our way through the intricate pre-Nicene patristic debates, and gave us an exciting introduction to contemporary trinitarian theology. The transcendental Thomism represented by Crowe and Lonergan was both invigorating and liberating. However, and this says more about me than about our professor or the books, I had no living and vibrant sense of the connection between the Trinity and the liturgy.

For me now, that connection means everything. Fr. Michael Paul Gallagher, SJ, who was in the class ahead of me, records his similar reflections on the course on the Trinity: "Putting this personally, I can clearly remember studying the Trinity in theology and indeed doing some ambitious essay on the doctrine as it evolved in the early centuries. But it was years later before it became spiritually alive for me and in fact has become one of the central enthusiasms of my faith."[2] I am sure that this experience is quite widespread and is a symptom of just how distant theology has been from liturgy and spirituality. When theology is packaged too neatly, it often loses connection with one's actual life. One theologian has recently put it like this: "Theology often does not read well….Its purpose is not fulfilled unless it is made as accessible as possible."[3]

The liturgy, the entire economy or history of salvation, indeed creation itself is about God's deifying us, about our participation in God. A splendid passage in Hans Urs von Balthasar's writing sets the stage for a consideration of the Trinity and the liturgy:

> We belong more to God than to ourselves; thus, we are also more in him than in ourselves. Ours is only the way leading to the eternal image of us that he bears within himself. This way is like a carpet rolled out from him to us, a scroll…"coming forth from the mouth of the Most High"—and we should, like children, learn how to copy it, how to trace the pre-scribed, pre-written characters that have been presented to us. The pre-scription, the law, is what Love has written out in advance, what Love presupposes and proposes to us that we might…become it.[4]

This passage has the merit of reminding us in a poetic and patristic vein of the fundamental insight of the old catechism question and answer: "Why did God make you?" "God made me to know him, love him and serve him in this life and to be happy with him forever in heaven." In a word, Balthasar here affirms that the purpose of life is divinization, our full creaturely participation in the life of God, initiated on earth, completed in heaven. It is essentially the dictum of Athanasius of Alexandria: "God became man so that man might become God." It is the backdrop to every Christian doctrine and to every liturgical action. The church, in all her actions and par excellence in her premier action of the liturgy, *is* the mechanism by which God is bringing about his purpose. And, of course, the God into whose life we are being drawn and divinized is the Trinity, Father, Son, and Holy Spirit. If we may take Balthasar's understanding as axiomatic, then we see this axiom played out in the history of the liturgy and in the contemporary understanding of the liturgy.

Encounter

First, however, we must grasp that the liturgy is primary theology. Encounter with the Triune God—before the Father, in the Son, through the Holy Spirit—is vastly more important than talk about such encounter, than theo-*logy*. In no way is this to denigrate the importance of doing theology, of secondary theology, but it is to acknowledge that, fundamentally, secondary theology is parasitic upon the experience of encounter with the Trinity. It is not to suggest naively that there is human experience without interpretation. The experience of a human person is already, ipso facto, involved in the act of interpretation, and necessarily so. To experience the liturgy is, therefore, to have some understanding, some interpretation, however limited, of what the liturgy is about. But in the order of being, as it were, experience of and encounter with God are primary, and theological reflection and interpretation are secondary. This is how the British Council of Churches put it in its document *The Forgotten Trinity*: "The primary form of this relationship (with God) is our worship, in which we are brought to God the Father through his Son and in his Spirit."[5]

The History of the Liturgy

In terms of baptism, trinitarian awareness begins with the Lord's command in St. Matthew's Gospel: "Go therefore and make disciples of all nations, baptizing them in the name of the Father and of the Son and of the Holy Spirit..." (Matt 28:19). Here in the Synoptic tradition, well before the end of the first century, is a formula setting Father, Son, and Spirit alongside one another as "equals," as it were. While the text clearly does not reflect the later language of consubstantiality/one in being, of the Son at Nicaea I (325 CE) and of the Spirit at Constantinople I (381 CE), nonetheless, the genesis of "one in being" is already present. Without prejudice to a careful analysis of the doctrinal tradition that led up to these foundational councils of the church, it may be said that more happened in terms of doctrine in the first few decades of the Christian era than in the next two centuries. The two centuries consequent upon the apostolic period unfold, tease out, challenge, and clarify the trinitarian understanding of God, but that it is there from the beginning seems incontestable. Cardinal Walter Kasper puts it as follows:

> The baptismal text (of Matthew 28:19) is not a novelty but simply gives concise expression to the basic trinitarian structure of the synoptic tradition and even of the entire New Testament. At the same time, the summary makes it clear that the trinitarian confession is not the result of theoretical reflection and speculation. Rather, it consummates the entire saving event which we appropriate in baptism. Consequently, it is baptism, that is, the act in which Christian existence is grounded which is the vital and sociological context...of the trinitarian confession.[6]

The eventual action, in which people become church and are embodied in Christ, is the primary vehicle at this early period for conveying and traditioning the awareness of God as Trinity. This tradition continues to be reflected in the *Didache*, an early Christian document written perhaps about 100 CE: "Now about baptism, here is the way it is performed: when you have recited all these instructions, baptize in the name of the Father and of the Son and of the Holy Spirit" (7:1). Just over one hundred years later in Rome, the presbyter Hippolytus witnesses to the same liturgical formula for baptism: "Do you believe in God the Father Almighty?...Do you believe in Jesus Christ the Son of God?...Do you believe in the Holy Spirit in the holy Church, and the resurrection of the flesh?"[7] Hippolytus's North African contemporary Tertullian of Carthage, in his *Against Praxeas*, testifies to the same theology: "[The Son] commands [the apostles] to baptize into the Father and the Son and the Holy Spirit, not into a unipersonal God. For not only once, but three times are we baptized into each of the Three Persons at each of the several names."[8]

In conjunction with baptism, liturgically and doctrinally, the Eucharist also provided the vital context for the acknowledgment of the Trinity. In Justin Martyr's description of the eucharistic prayer, written about 150 CE, we read the following: "The (presider) takes the bread and wine, and sends up praise and glory to the Father of all in the name of the Son and of the Holy Spirit, and gives thanks at some length that we have been deemed worthy of these things from him."[9] Hippolytus, some sixty-five years later in the same Roman community, provides a similar troping of the Trinity: "We render thanks to you, O God, through your beloved child Jesus Christ, whom in the last times you sent to us as a Savior and Redeemer and Angel of your will....He was made flesh and was manifested as your Son, being born of the Holy Spirit and the Virgin...."[10] One could go on and on to provide an impressive catena of patristic liturgical and doctrinal formulas that make the same basic point: God is Trinity, and nothing less than this will do for those moments in which this God is addressed in worship and prayer. One could conclude that the trinitarian articulations of the councils of Nicaea and Constantinople were but the logical or reflective outcomes of the constancy of trinitarian worship. *Lex orandi, lex credendi.* Let us, however, move on to recognize how the Triune God is knit into the liturgical year.

The Liturgical Year

The church's prayer is woven around the warp and woof of the liturgical year. Every year the Christian community relives the event of Jesus Christ, that is, the divine economy of Christ and the Spirit.[11] Advent focuses on the coming of Christ, both at Christmas and the Parousia. The season ends with the Baptism of the Lord, in the Gospel traditions a decidedly and explicitly trinitarian event. The Easter season commences on Ash Wednesday, proceeds along the weeks of Lent through the Easter Vigil, and comes to its term on Pentecost Sunday, celebrating the coming of the Holy Spirit.

The remainder of the liturgical year is Ordinary Time, the time of growth in the ecclesial Body of Christ, centered on each Sunday's celebration of the Paschal Mystery. The liturgical color is green, the color of growth and new life. Special feasts throughout the year commemorate those holy women and men whose canonized example offers the church icons of the Christian life at its best. Not icons, however, of imitative human endeavor, but icons translucent of the Paschal Mystery, human persons utterly conformed to the Christ.

Finally, there is the three-year lectionary cycle. The scriptures tell the story of God's coming among us, of his continued Spirit-led guidance, and of the fulfillment to come. The scriptures nourish the memory and keep the hope alive of those events that constitute the Triune deification of this Christian community, what we call the life of grace.

The Celebration of the Eucharist

The Eucharist is a trinitarian event from beginning to end. The celebration begins with the Sign of the Cross: "In the name of the Father, and of the Son and of the Holy Spirit." It ends on the same note with the blessing of the priest: "May almighty God bless you, the Father, the Son and the Holy Spirit." Here is a eucharistic-trinitarian inclusion: at the outset the trinitarian invitation to become more fully trinified, at the end trinitarian mission to be in our particular circumstances what has been celebrated. This inclusion sets up the ritual boundaries in the celebration of the Eucharist of our divinization. The great hymn of praise, the Gloria, takes up again the trinitarian note sounded at the beginning and weaves it into a symphony of praise. All of the eucharistic prayers have a trinitarian shape, but it is perhaps clearest in Eucharistic Prayer IV, celebrating the entire sweep of salvation history from beginning to end. If the whole of salvation history is proclaimed, and if the economic Trinity is the immanent Trinity in Karl Rahner's great insight, then we should expect to find the Trinity continually and explicitly iterated in this prayer.

The Trinity is celebrated in the act of praise that unfolds after the Sanctus: "We give you praise, Father most holy, / for you are great / and you have fashioned all your works / in wisdom and in love." The initial address is to the Father, but from the Love that the Father in the Son is sent: "And you so loved the world, Father most holy, / that in the fullness of time / you sent your Only Begotten Son to be our Savior." The human becoming of the Son is through the agency of the Holy Spirit: he was "made incarnate by the Holy Spirit and born of the Virgin Mary...." Mention of the Holy Spirit enables the transition to the first epiclesis: "Therefore, O Lord, we pray: / may this same Holy Spirit / graciously sanctify these offerings, / that they may become / the Body and Blood of our Lord Jesus Christ...." As Raymond Moloney, SJ, puts it in his commentary on the eucharistic prayers, "The work of the Spirit prepares for the coming of the Word in our liturgy just as he once prepared for his coming in the womb of Mary....Implicitly this canon is saying to us that the history of salvation is recapitulated in every Eucharist. Every Mass is the Trinity drawing us into its life."[12] There is a further dimension to this trinitarian divinization

11

articulated in Eucharistic Prayer IV. The Lord is asked to remember all those who form his Body through the activity of the Spirit: "Lord, remember now / all for whom we offer this sacrifice...." Included here are "all who seek you with a sincere heart."

The process of divinization is signified in the church through the Holy Spirit but is not necessarily confined there. As Enrico Mazza has it, "This phrase of the intercessions [in the eucharistic prayer] makes movingly present in our Eucharist all those who have not yet discovered the greatness of the Lord but are journeying toward him, even if without their knowledge...."[13] Finally, the work of the Holy Spirit is seen in the climax of salvation history: "There [in your kingdom], with the whole of creation, / freed from the corruption of sin and death, / may we glorify you through Christ our Lord...." The end-time is like a great cosmic liturgy in which the whole world will be transfigured and transformed by the Holy Spirit. The trinitarian *exitus/outward movement* of creation reaches its term in the *reditus/return* to the Trinity.

Ecumenism, Liturgy, Trinity

In his 1997 presidential address to the American Theological Society, the Methodist liturgical and ecumenical theologian Geoffrey Wainwright has shown how central the liturgy has been for trinitarian awareness in the ecumenical movement.[14] Judging that the recovery of the Paschal Mystery has probably been the most outstanding achievement of the liturgical movement, Wainwright goes on to note its trinitarian dimensions. These come to the fore in both scripture and liturgy. In scripture we read that Christ offered himself to God through the eternal Spirit (Heb 9:15) and that the Father raised the Son from the dead by the Holy Spirit (Rom 1:3f; 8:11). In liturgy the Paschal Mystery is celebrated centrally in the Easter Vigil, the high point of the liturgical year, and Wainwright recognizes that "many Protestant churches have introduced their own versions of the occasion."[15] At the Easter Vigil baptism in the name of the Trinity is celebrated, baptismal promises in the trinitarian-creedal form are made, the Eucharist is offered, and thus communion in and with the Trinity takes place. But this trinitarian rediscovery is not, of course, peculiar to the Easter Vigil, nor to the ongoing celebration of the Eucharist in the churches. It is also to be found in key texts of the ecumenical movement. Without attempting to be exhaustive, Wainwright goes on to point up in considerable detail its presence in many ecumenical documents, especially from the Faith and Order Commission of the World Council of Churches, in particular the Lima Statement (1982) on "Baptism, Eucharist and Ministry."[16]

If one turns to the ecumenical dialogue between the Orthodox churches and Catholicism, the Trinity is omnipresent, as one would expect, in those documents that have to do with the liturgy. Arguably the most egregious example is to be found in the Munich Statement and the Bari Statement. This Munich Statement carries the title "The Mystery of the Church and of the Eucharist in the Light of the Mystery of the Holy Trinity." In paragraph 6 we read, "Taken as a whole, the Eucharistic celebration makes present the trinitarian mystery of the church. In it one passes from hearing the Word, culminating in the proclamation of the Gospel, the apostolic announcing of the Word made flesh, to the thanksgiving offered to the Father, then the memorial of the sacrifice of Christ and to communion in him thanks to the prayer of the epiclesis uttered in faith." The entire statement, along with the Bari Statement (1987) and the Valamo Statement (1988), offers a very fine synthesis of Trinity-liturgy-church.

Conclusion

Christian liturgy is necessarily trinitarian. It is trinitarian in its structure, in its history, in its contemporary expression. Both Catholics and Christians from any church tradition that subscribes to historic Christianity will affirm this. But perhaps the real pastoral issue is to find those key moments not so much that reemphasize the obvious trinitarian nexus of the liturgy but that invite deeper personal appropriation of the mystery. Such key moments seem to me to be both homiletical and catechetical.

Preaching the Trinity, finding trinitarian connections in the lectionary offerings, dwelling on such readings almost in the manner of *lectio divina* are essential. As a homilist I recognize experientially the difficulty and challenge of the task. That fine Dominican homilist Geoffrey Preston opens a homily on Trinity Sunday with these words: "On Trinity Sunday the preacher is expected to do something towards elucidating this conundrum (of the Trinity), although from past experience he will probably only make the darkness doubly dark."[17] Preston is right. It is difficult to avoid making the darkness of the Trinity doubly dark, but perhaps for a preacher a good start could be made not only by saturating himself in the scriptural readings but also by examining the trinitarian homilies of preachers like Geoffrey Preston, OP, and Walter Burghardt, SJ. A careful study of their homilies, and other such homilies, would reveal graceful ways in which we might move forward.[18]

In terms of catechesis one could not do better than to study the exemplary trinitarian theology of the sacraments as expressed in the *Catechism of the Catholic Church*. How we pray shapes how we believe. The sacraments, as the premier form of our prayer lives, are a paradigm of trinitarian awareness. To work through that section of the *Catechism* would be rewarding for anyone concerned with catechesis. If as a church we tried to make our preaching and teaching more carefully trinitarian, then we might move to a more pervasive and perduring appropriation of the Trinity as the shape of our liturgy and of our lives.

Worship and the Catholic Imagination: Church as Sacred Space

*Religious behavior, like language, is not the product of ratiocination
....It is rooted in social processes. It is because people exult and
lament, sing for joy, bewail their sins and so on, that they are able,
eventually, to have thoughts about God. Worship is not the result
but the precondition of believing in God....At any rate, when
people no longer praise God there will be no need for theology.*

Fergus Kerr, OP[1]

Acknowledging Worship as a Dimension of Religion

We saw in the first chapter the absolute centrality of the Trinity
to liturgy. As we set out to explore worship and the Catholic imagination, it may be helpful to begin by looking briefly at the phenomenon of worship as such. It is simply a fact that worship is
part and parcel of the global phenomenon of religion. The words
of Scottish Dominican Fergus Kerr that open this chapter affirm
the centrality of worship for religion and make exactly the right
emphasis: "When people no longer praise God there will be no
need for theology." Wherever religious people are found, there
they worship. It is to the credit of the philosopher of religion
Ninian Smart (1927–2001) that, at a time when philosophy of

religion was largely given over to an exploration of arguments for the existence of God and perhaps the problem of evil and suffering, he came to an understanding of religion that firmly situated worship and ritual as essential to its understanding. Smart believed that there were various dimensions of religion that had to be taken into account if one were ever to reach any adequate grasp of the phenomenon, and central to these dimensions was ritual or worship. In the first edition (1969) of his justly famous *The Religious Experience of Mankind* he situates ritual as the very first of his dimensions of religion. "Religion tends in part to express itself through such rituals: through worship, prayers, offerings, and the like."[2] Ritual need not be elaborate, like a liturgy of the Orthodox churches, or a Pontifical High Mass. It may be something as simple as closing one's eyes in prayer. But, whatever particular expression it has, ritual is fundamental to religion.

There is, if you will, an "outer" and "inner" meaning to ritual. The outer is what might be seen, heard, and perhaps smelled by an outsider (think of incense!), one who is not a participant in a particular religious faith. The inner is the contact made by the religious participant in and through ritual with God, the realm of the divine, or, as Smart puts it in its broadest description, "the invisible world." The inner and outer come together in the liturgical architecture, the liturgical shape of the church building. If you like, the building is the message! The building is the message along with all that happens in the building. One cannot adequately be had without the other. Everything about the building and the events in it speaks its meaning.

The Space of the Body of Christ

Perhaps the first thing to say about a church building is that it is a powerful local sign of transcendence, of the reality of God, of heaven as God's space. Often churches are much higher than other buildings in the immediate environment. As Robert Barron puts it, "The dramatic verticality of the buildings compels the gaze of the spirit upward."[3] Why upward? Because "upward" for us is a sign, perhaps a natural sign, of God's immensity and transcendence.

However, this God whose sign the verticality of the building is, is so much more than the important word *transcendent* can identify. Churches remind us of the immensity of God, of the intensity of God, of God as sheerly present and inviting us to communion. When a worshiper or even a visitor is invited by the doors of a church swinging open, she or he is moving into a mystical space, tense with invitation to self-awareness and divine communion. The door to mystical communion with God swings open in the lives of everyone, at least sometimes. These mystical moments are moments when we have an overwhelming sense of well-being, an experience that we would like to prolong. Anthropologist Margaret Visser describes superbly what happens when we move into the space of the church, the space of many cumulative mystical moments: "A church is a recognition, in stone and wood and brick, of spiritual awakenings. It nods, to each individual person....It constitutes a collective memory of spiritual insights, of thousands of mystical moments. A church reminds us of what we have known. And it tells us that the possibility of the door swinging open again remains."[4] That phrase, "the church *nods*," is very fine. The building is not just stone and brick, the building is invitation, and so it nods to the worshiper, or to the visitor.

Consider, too, this passage from the Dominican liturgical theologian Jean Corbon:

> Human beings have always felt their houses, their homes, to be prolongations of their own bodies, a kind of second space (after their garments) for their persons. A house humanizes space, makes it habitable, makes it personal....In Christ the Father performs this marvelous adaptation in a way that is beyond all possible expectations: we become his dwelling place by taking on the form of his Son's body. This configuration is given visible symbolization in cruciform churches: when the

people of God assemble there, they take on the form of
the crucified Christ who overcame death....[5]

Corbon takes Visser further. Not only does the church nod to us,
inviting mystical moments, but it also acts as a kind of mirror helping us to see who we are actually as the Body of Christ, or who we
are potentially as the Body of Christ. In other words, this space is
our home, our home as the Body of Christ. This space is where we
worship God, acknowledge God as our source and our final end.
This space is most especially associated with our becoming more
fully and more perfectly the Body of our Lord Jesus Christ. We take
on the form of the crucified and risen Christ. When we visit the
church for prayer, and especially for corporate worship, we are not
only reminded of this fact in a psychological way. The fact is rein-
forced by our very being here and by our very doing here.

Msgr. Francis Mannion writes,

> Material place symbolically amplifies the liturgical action,
> and the liturgy, in turn, draws into itself the spatial and
> material....To hold that a church building is simply a
> functional dwelling is to imply that divine presence is
> operative no more in a liturgical building than anywhere
> else....Liturgical buildings, on the other hand, should not
> be conceived of as sacral places, that is, places that limit,
> contain or bind divine presence and action. God does not
> dwell exclusively in church buildings.[6]

Is it possible to pray and to worship anywhere? Yes, of course it is.
Do we need church buildings in which to pray and worship, buildings like the cathedral? Yes, of course we do. Why? Msgr. Mannion's
words help to explain: "Material place amplifies the liturgy, and the
liturgy draws into itself the spatial and material." The Catholic faith
is very materialistic, not in the sense of money and materialism, not
in the sense of consumerism. There is another meaning for *materialism,* a more literal sense, the sense that for Catholics matter matters!
Catholics are not Gnostics, for whom matter was of little or no con-

cern. Matter has come from God—the doctrine of creation—and matter is being drawn by God to himself at the end of time. Matter is holy. The church building is holy because matter is holy and what people do there is holy. Mannion goes on to say, "I would argue that...the holiness of the church building and the holiness of the people of God are mutually generative and interactively constitutive."[7] Mannion exemplifies here a typically Catholic way of doing theology, not so much in either/or terms as in both-and terms. Perhaps we could put it like this. Church buildings are trying to speak to us, trying to tell us that we are made for more than the ordinary. We are made for the extraordinary, for extraordinary mystical communion with God. When people come into the church, and this is true of visitors and of us whose home this building is, they are listening to the building. Drawing again on Margaret Visser:

> The building is trying to speak; not listening to what it has to say is a form of barbarous inattention, like admiring a musical instrument while caring nothing for music....All of the church's "language" exists to help you (encounter the mystery of God and so encounter your deepest self), to get your mind humming and to make you receptive....A church is there to remind you, to teach you to pay attention, and to awaken the poetry in your soul. It gives you exercise in responding....For anyone who is not spiritually allergic to churches, to walk into a beautiful church is to encounter understanding, to hear echoes of the soul's own experiences of epiphany. Such stimulus and concurrence need not involve anything theological. It can be a matter simply of sunlight striking through colored glass and dappling the wall opposite, of the smell of flowers and lingering hints of incense, of the silent cold of stone, of movements of the soul that respond directly to columns, arches, domes, coloring, and carving, or to the memory of the people who have filled this building in the past....It's a hole in the hard walls of the rackety everyday, a reassur-

ance that, thanks to the care and attention of my fellow human beings, a place has been made ready for silent contact with something enormous, something present, for anyone who wants it.[8]

That is, quite simply, a marvelous passage, a passage that lends itself to *lectio divina* again and again. The holiness of the Christian assembly and the holiness of the liturgical building are not oppositional or in competition but are harmoniously related and mutually constitutive; the church building is both *the house of God* and *the house of the church* and, if attention is carefully paid to what the building is saying, *a potential house for humankind*.

We come to the church to worship God and to be made better and more fully what we are by God's grace, the holy Body of Christ. "Every celebration of the liturgy is geared to that lived liturgy in which each instant of life should become a 'moment' of grace. The liturgy cannot be lived at each moment, however, unless it is celebrated at certain moments."[9] The well-known liturgical theologian Robert Taft, SJ, uses a marvelous image to describe what the liturgy does. He asks us to call to mind Michelangelo's creation of Adam in the Sistine Chapel in Rome. God the Father is reaching down with his outstretched hand toward Adam. Adam is lying down reaching up with his outstretched hand toward God. The space between their fingers is the space of the liturgy, the space of our worship. Through this liturgy God is drawing us literally into his own life, into communion with himself, to be the within of God's Within. When the sacraments are celebrated, when the Liturgy of the Hours is prayed here in this building, that's what is happening! God is divinizing us! That's what is happening in this little space! The little space of the liturgy, the little space of our persons, in the space of the church.

The Church: Heaven in Stone and Glass

"Heaven" is the point of our full and final divinization, beatitude, vision—all these terms are in reality synonyms for God's completion of us. Thus, Robert Barron's description of a cathedral—and it can be said equally of an ordinary church—is very apt: "heaven in stone and glass."[10] Heaven is God's "place," with the angels, with the saints. The fact that God is not alone signifies that God wants company. In a sense, God is Company, God is a Communion of Persons: Father, Son, and Holy Spirit, the Trinity of our first chapter. That's why our entire liturgy begins with a sign of the Holy Company of God, the Sign of the Cross: in Barron's words, "We come to the heart of it. God is not a monolith, not an undifferentiated unity, and not a 'thing' dumbly at one with itself. Rather, God is a play of relationality, a *communio* of persons…. Once the community has gathered itself for prayer, the liturgy proper begins with the Sign of the Cross, the invocation of the *communio* which is God."[11] "In the name of the Father, and of the Son, and of the Holy Spirit." In the name of Heaven!

The Communion that is God is not content to remain in God-self. Rather, God goes outside himself to create companionship—the angels, everything that is, and us. Look around the church. We are immediately reminded of this. Look at the images of the angels. Of course, the depictions we see are just that—pictures. Angels are real but not embodied like us. They surround us—our notion of guardian angels, an expression of God's love for us, and God's custodial care. They are around us, especially in the liturgy. We sing the song of the angels from the sixth chapter of the Book of Isaiah in the liturgy: "Holy, holy, holy, Lord God of hosts. Heaven and earth are full of your glory. Hosanna in the highest…." "The angels…compel our spirits (crippled by the cold empiricism of the Enlightenment) out past the world of nature, past the cosmos itself, into the forecourts of God's house."[12] In the Rule of St. Benedict, the monks are instructed not to fidget, not to cough and splutter, not to pick at themselves during the singing of the Liturgy of the Hours—because God's angels are in front and all around them! This leads the great patristic theologian Origen of Alexandria to say that there is "a double church present, one of men, and the other of angels."[13] Though invisible, though we may be unaware, there is a dynamism between the world of the angels and the world of humankind. Again, using Barron's words: "Their world and ours—though separated by a great ontological gulf—nevertheless interpenetrate, prayer and loving concern moving in both directions...."[14] Needless to say, of course, this interpenetration of angels and human beings cannot be demonstrated in any ordinary sense of the word. Without getting locked into superstition or sheer fantasy, however, there is an interpenetration, and when one habitually submits to this acknowledgment, wonderful things happen. To illustrate further takes us into the realm of self-revelation or autobiography, and that's not where we are going.

What about the saints? The big saints and the little saints. The big saints? Those whose sanctity we celebrate in the yearly round of feasts, whose names we call out at the Easter Vigil, at baptism, confirmation, holy orders. They form our family album. That's why we have images of the saints around our churches. As a deacon, I love especially that moment at the Easter Vigil when the congregation sings out the Litany of the Saints, and those about to be sanctified—that is, baptized—walk through our midst to the baptismal font. Sheer grace! Especially Our Lady Mary, first among the saints. The little saints? Those who have gone before us marked with the sign of faith: deceased members of our own families, deceased members of our parish families. Our hope and rightful expectation is that they have come into God's holy presence, into God's communion, healed and whole, brought home to our Father's house. We are never on our own, even if sometimes it feels like that. We are surrounded by the angels and saints.

The Church, the Sacraments, and Communion

It's all about communion—our communion in the Communion that is God and our communion in, with, and through one another as the Body of Christ, and with the entire human race. Our anatomy as Christ's Body marks out the space of the church building. Catholicism is incarnational, materialistic, to do with things.

This is what Fr. Andrew Greeley calls the "Catholic imagination." He writes:

> Catholics live in an enchanted world, a world of statues
> and holy water, stained-glass and votive candles, saints
> and religious medals, rosary beads and holy pictures.
> But these Catholic paraphernalia are mere hints of a
> deeper and more pervasive religious sensibility which
> inclines Catholics to see the Holy lurking in creation.
> As Catholics, we find our houses and our world
> haunted by a sense that the objects, events, and persons
> of daily life are revelations of grace.[15]

This is why the sacraments, and indeed sacramentals, are so important to Catholics. The sacraments are the anatomy of Christ's Body, our anatomy as the Body of Christ.

Most Catholics will not read big books of theology but will remain attracted to and by the sacraments and the sacramentals of the church. This is how Andrew Greeley puts it:

> If the high tradition is to be found in theology books and
> the documents of the councils, and the papacy, and the
> various hierarchies of the world, the popular tradition is
> to be found in the rituals, the art, the music, the archi-
> tecture, the devotions, the stories of ordinary people. If
> the former can be stated concisely at any given time in
> creeds which are collections of prose propositions, the
> latter is fluidly, amorphously, and elusively expressed in
> stories. Prosaic people that we are, we members of the
> Catholic elite are inclined to believe that the real
> Catholicism is that of the high tradition. Doctrine and
> dogma are more important than experience and narra-
> tive....The Christmas crib is popular Catholicism; the
> decrees of [the Council of] Chalcedon are high
> Catholicism. The same story of God among us is told by
> both, the same fundamental reality of our faith is dis-

closed by both, the same rumor of angels is heard in both. Which, however, has more impact on the lives of ordinary Catholics? Anyone who thinks *homoousios* (consubstantial/one in being) is more important to ordinary folk than the Madonna and her Child is incurably prosaic—besides being wrong![16]

This affirmation of Greeley's has a certain infallible feel to it! The entire layout of the church speaks this popular tradition of Andrew Greeley. The entire layout of the church—we've already looked at some of the architecture and art—speaks the mystery of Christ, or better, speaks to ourselves as and in the mystery of Christ, inviting us more deeply into that mystery that we already are.

The large space in the church is known as the nave. The word *nave* comes from the Latin word *navis*, which means "ship." In antiquity, "always the sea is presented as changeable and dangerous, the Mediterranean being peculiarly prone to storms: the sea is a major metaphor in Greek literature for fate and necessity, or circumstances all the wise beyond human control."[17] Understandably, then, a ship becomes a symbol of safety in the no less turbulent sea of human living. Moreover, a ship is going somewhere; there is a sense of direction. And so early Christians thought of the church as a ship, a *navis*, a nave. Citing and paraphrasing the patristic author, Hippolytus of Rome, Margaret Visser continues:

> Like a ship, the church carried people of many different origins; Christ was the pilot; the Roman double rudder was "the two Testaments." Sails and rigging were "stretched out" like life for others or like Christ himself embracing the church. The rigging was a cosmic ladder, a "way up" towards God. Human technology—the craft of shipbuilders, sailing by the stars, understanding the winds, the plotting of routes—enables the ship to arrive where it wants to go, just as the church is led by God's Word, by grace and response, by wisdom, and by fixing its sights on its goal. The point of the ship metaphor…

is above all movement forward, towards the world's destiny, and also towards both end and fulfillment for the individual.[18]

All of this symbolism contained in the nave!

The central liturgical focus in any Catholic church is the altar, symbolizing Christ, the ultimate Gift, given as Eucharist. The "Rite of the Dedication of the Church and an Altar" helps us to realize this centrality: "Here may your children, gathered around your altar, celebrate the memorial of the Paschal Lamb, and be fed at the table of Christ's word and Christ's body" (par. 62). It is at the altar that the priest, assisted by the deacon, in the person of Christ the head of the Body of Christ, celebrates the Eucharist in and through which our transformation into Christ is both signified and effected. This leads Jean Corbon to observe, "The altar is in effect the point of convergence for all the lines in the space that is the church."[19] The Eucharist is the central mechanism of what we might call our Trinification, our being drawn into the Divine Communion.

In close and essential relationship to the altar is the ambo, the Table of the Word, from which the word of God is proclaimed. "[The ambo] should reflect the dignity of God's Word and be a key reminder to the people that in the Mass the Table of God's Word and of Christ's Body is placed before them" (*Lectionary of the Mass*, par. 62). Encountering Christ present, the word speaking to us in the Liturgy of the Word, and consuming Christ present in the liturgy of the Eucharist enfolds us in the communion of the Trinity. "We become the one whom we have received and in whom the Spirit has transformed us. The fruit of the Eucharist, to which all the power of the river of life is directed, is communion…with the Blessed Trinity."[20]

Now we move on to the baptismal font. If we are fed and nourished at the Table of the Word and the Eucharist as daughters and sons in the Son, as children of the Father, we are born into this privileged condition when the waters of baptism break over our heads at the womb of Mother Church, the baptismal font.

Baptism may never be dissociated from the sacrament of confirmation. They are inextricably bound together and inextricably bound to the Eucharist, the terminal point of the sacred process of initiation. Our Trinification, our communion in the Communion of God, gets under way.

The sacrament of penance and reconciliation, what we have traditionally called "confession" and its place the confessional, the place of forgiveness, where our obdurate refusal to live as Christ's Body, to submit to the process of Trinification, is both acknowledged and healed. I always find the words of George Herbert so helpful here, from his poem "Discipline":

> Though I fail, I weep;
> though I halt in pace, yet I creep to the throne of grace.

That weeping and halting and creeping are so essential to human growth, and absolutely essential to relationship with God in the Body of Christ. Can we not acknowledge our faults, or failings, and our sins privately to God, without going through the sacrament of penance and reconciliation? Of course, we can! But the sacrament exists not to make it more difficult for us, but in a very real sense to make it easier for us. This is how Jean Corbon puts it, and puts it quite radically:

> It is true, of course, that on the altar of our hearts we can ceaselessly offer the bread of tears for our sins and that the fire of the Spirit can inflame us ever anew. But who can deny that there are moments in our lives when our accumulated rejections and ruptures are such that we cannot honestly avoid confessing our sins and being reconciled to the community? "Insofar as you did this to one of the least of these brothers of mine, you did it to me": this statement holds for giving them death as well as giving them life....Every sin, even the most

26

secret, has inflicted a wound on the body; the member must therefore be healed in the body.[21]

This is a truly ecclesial, truly corporate understanding of sin and of the sacrament of penance and reconciliation. Hence the importance of the public celebration of the sacrament. We have wounded the body, and the body needs to heal that wound.

Next comes the ambry, a public place for depositing the sacred oils used for anointing catechumens, the sick, and for those receiving the sacraments of baptism, confirmation, and holy orders. The visibility of the holy oils is important for our continual awareness of our being communion moving finally toward the Divine Communion. This is especially the case with the oil of the sick. The oil of the sick and the sacrament of the anointing of the sick console when we are ill, yet they also remind us that even when ill we do not cease to be this holy Body, and so we are summoned to witness to Christ and his grace.

Marriage is normally celebrated in the church, in the sanctuary. "Make of these hands one hand, make of these hearts one heart, make of these lives one life"—lines from *West Side Story*—marriage thus is an icon of Christ-Church until death. Marriage too is sacrament of communion. "The new element in a specifically sacramental marriage transforms the spouses first of all; beyond all opposition between the spouses and all thought of superiority on the one or other side, the relationship of the two can be constantly renewed so as to share in the transparency of the union of Christ and the Church."[22]

Finally, the sacrament of holy orders, in which bishop and priest and deacon are ordained as ministers of communion. The bishop is the one in whom the fullness of this service to communion exists. The bishop, and with him the priest, is "in the person of Christ the Head," and the deacon is "in the person of Christ the Servant." The purpose of ordination is to serve the communion of all in Christ, building up the Body of Christ, the better to witness and serve.

Liturgy Celebrated and Liturgy Lived

When the liturgy is celebrated in this quite literally "wonderful" building of the church, in all its different sacramental manifestations, we are made fully alive. "When we celebrate the liturgy we participate in an intense and unique way in the totality of our life, in its adorable Lord....We truly 'live' during the celebration....None of us is ever so much himself or herself, nor is the church so much itself, nor are the universe and history so exalted in hope of glory, as when the liturgy is being celebrated...."[23] It hardly needs to be pointed out, however, that the meaning of all that happens in the church's liturgy is verified in living. The test of authentic worship is, as the Orthodox would have it, the liturgy after the liturgy! What has been celebrated is tested and verified in the living of our lives. "During the 'moments' of celebration the intense gift of the Holy Spirit causes us to experience the church; it manifests the church, causes it to grow, and transforms it into the body of Christ....The mystery of God's communion with human beings then needs to be tested in actuality and by ourselves: We have become the body of Christ: are we going to live as his body?"[24] All liturgical celebrations end with a blessing. But the blessing is in reality not just the terminal point of the celebration, but "a sending forth, a mission. Let us now live in him whom we have received and let us share him with others."[25]

When all is said and done, the liturgy is about our corporate and personal transformation so that we may be corporately and personally transforming agents in the liturgy of life. God draws us to himself in communion in our drawing others to communion, in letting our hearts become the agents of transformation after the liturgy. The altar of the heart goes out to meet the altar of the world.

3

The Holy Scriptures:
Through a Poetical Lens

The Word assembles the Church for his incarnation in her.
Alexander Schmemann[1]

I myself have been reading the Scriptures for over forty years, and at every reading I am astonished to find them utterly new; at every reading I experience the jolt to mind and feelings that stirs a sense of human values and puts me in touch with the values of God.
Carlo M. Martini[2]

The scriptures, and especially the New Testament, were written to be proclaimed in liturgy, when Christians were gathered together for worship and most especially the Eucharist. St. Paul, for example, wrote his letters to be read before the worshiping congregations at Rome and Corinth and other places that he had visited. The Gospels were drawn up with similar audiences in mind. These writings were not written primarily for individual study—for it is unlikely that many of the earliest Christians were literate or had their own copies of the texts—but in order to form the community around the revelation of God, the proclaimed word of scripture. It is only in the church and primarily in the context of its prayer and worship that the Bible finds its providential place and meaning.[3]

This is why all the sacraments of the Catholic Church are celebrated with the word, with the proclamation of holy scripture. Scripture and sacrament together make for communion with God. One author recently put it like this: "The mystery of God's plan to reunite creation with God's own existence is embodied in Christ, discerned in the Scriptures, and sacramentally enacted in the Eucharistic community."[4] The "discernment of God's plan in the scriptures" is the concern of this chapter. If God's plan is to unite us with himself, to bring us into communion with the Divine Communion, centered in the Eucharist, then the scriptures are profoundly eucharistic.

George Herbert and Holy Scripture

George Herbert is one of my favorite poets. I know few more pleasing ways into a eucharistic appreciation of holy scripture than two poems of this Anglican priest-poet and eucharistic mystic George Herbert (1593–1633), both poems with the title "The Holy Scriptures."

The Holy Scriptures I

O Book! Infinite sweetness! Let my heart
   Suck every letter and a honey gain,
   Precious for any grief in any part;
To clear the breast, to mollify all pain.
Thou art all health, health thriving till it make
   A full eternity: thou art a mass
   Of strange delights, where we may wish and take.
Ladies, look here; this is the thankful glass,
That mends the looker's eyes: this is the well
   That washes what it shows. Who can endear
   Thy praise too much? Thou art heavn's lidger here,
Working against the states of death and hell.
   Thou art joy's handsel: heav'n lies flat in thee,
   Subject to every mounter's bended knee.

The scriptures are personified and addressed: "O Book!" They are God's word to us, a word that nourishes and sustains. The image of sucking almost suggests God as a mother, whose breasts are

30

holy scripture, where the heart may "suck every letter and a honey gain." The image may also be that of the bee, making honey from sucking at the flowers. It is a scriptural image itself, as in Psalm 119:103: "How sweet are your words unto my taste, / sweeter than honey to my mouth." Whichever image it is, and one does not necessarily have to choose one over the other, God sustains and nourishes us through his sweet words in scripture.

This scriptural nourishment helps us to overcome grief, to clear the breast, to deal with pain because "Thou art all health, health thriving till it make a full eternity." The nourishment and medicinal value of scripture help us to heal and grow, to thrive until we reach "a full eternity" in heaven. If the purpose of life is to reach full and consummate communion in and with God, this communion is begun not only in and through the sacraments of the church, centered on the Eucharist, but also in the holy scriptures. Then we are fed with the word, the word of God's own life. Notice Herbert's expression: "Thou art a mass of strange delights, where we may wish and take." There may be a strangeness to scripture that may delight, or perhaps even may challenge, but this is something to which we shall return later.

Herbert now changes the image to that of a mirror. "Ladies, look here; this is the thankful glass, that mends the looker's eyes." Our vision is so often unhealthy. When we look at ourselves in a glass, in a mirror, if we are honest, we do not see "all health." We see sickness and ill health. When, however, we look at scripture as in a mirror, we see the full health that may be ours if we take its medicinal properties into ourselves. Scripture "will mend the looker's eyes."

Slightly changing the image, scripture is like a well in which we see our reflection, but again, this reflection is not perfectly healthy: it is disfigured by the un-love that we are. This well of scripture, however, "washes what it shows." It has the power to cleanse us of all that is un-love, if we will.

The image of scripture changes even more now. Scripture is "heavn's lidger here," that is, here on earth. *Lidger* means "ledger," with the double sense of "resident ambassador" or "register" (in the sense of *book*). Scripture is the ambassador of heaven, heaven's representative on earth. An ambassador does not speak his own words. He speaks the words of his king or queen. His is the voice, certainly, but the words, the message comes from the one who sent him. Scripture is God's ambassador, speaking God's words to us.

At the same time, it is heaven's register of forces and goods, ready to help us wage war against death and hell. With the register of heaven's supports found in scripture, we shall be successful in the conflict. This not so much a cosmic conflict for Herbert as the conflict within ourselves, the moral and spiritual conflict or struggle for real and lasting spiritual health. All the means are found in the register of scripture.

Scripture is also "joy's handsel." *Handsel* means a first installment, a down payment, with the full payment to come in the future. It is a promise of greater than itself. I like to think of joy as both subjective and objective. "Joy" is God's name. Scripture is the first installment of the joy that is God, in whom we find the real en-joyment that cannot be taken from us. This is the joy begun on earth that comes to final fruition in heaven. At the same time and because of this, scripture gives us joy *now*, as in its reading we anticipate the joy that is God-to-come. Scripture is the sacrament of God's joy-full presence for the reader here and now.

Once more, the image of scripture changes. Scripture becomes a map of heaven: "heav'n lies flat in thee." A map is flat as it manifests to us the reality of an unknown territory. Scripture is the map of heaven. As we wind our way in pilgrimage toward heaven, we need this map for direction and guidance so as to arrive at our destination and not get lost, and not find ourselves lost literally. Scripture is the down payment of heaven, "Joy's handsel," the dwelling place of God, and before our God and king we should bend the knee, the very last line of the poem.

The Holy Scriptures II

O that I knew how all thy lights combine,
    And the configurations of their glory!
    Seeing not only how each verse doth shine,
But all the constellations of the story.
This verse marks that, and both do make a motion
    Unto a third, that ten leaves off doth lie:
    Then as dispersed herbs do watch a potion,
These three make up some Christian's destiny:
Such are thy secrets, which my life makes good,
    And comments on thee: for in ev'rything
    Thy words do find me out, and parallels bring,
And in another make me understood
    Stars are poor books, and oftentimes do miss:
    This book of stars lights to eternal bliss.

In this second poem, as Herbert gazes at the starry night sky, he thinks once again of the holy scriptures. Scripture lights up God's story, the narrative of the scriptures, just as the stars light up God's sky. As one star leads to another, and one constellation leads to another, so one verse or one chapter or one book of holy scripture leads to another and another and another. While each verse of scripture has its own integral meaning, it is the canonical whole of scripture that provides us with the story of God's coming among us and of God's ways with us. In this fashion, without doing any injustice to the individual meanings of the individual parts, we get a sense of God's whole story.

Next, Herbert turns to another metaphor, that of the herbalist working in his pharmacy. The herbalist picks up this herb and that as he mixes them into a medicinal potion to make someone well. All the verses of scripture are so many herbs that provide different healing remedies for what ails Christians. Not only that: the scriptures find us out and challenge us to make our words and our ways more scriptural. Yet again, Herbert changes his metaphor. Now he thinks of the mariner using the constellations and stars of the heavens to guide his ship through the seas. Mistakes can be made. The book of stars that comprises the holy scriptures is, however, a sure guide that lights up the route to heaven.

Scripture on Scripture

In these two poems, George Herbert provides us with a commentary on the power of God's holy word. The sheer power and dynamism of holy scripture is set out within the scriptures themselves. Let's take just a few examples. First, Deuteronomy 8:3, a passage that is cited by our Blessed Lord himself in Matthew 4:4: "One does not live by bread alone, / but by every word that comes from the mouth of God." Just as bread stands as a symbol of the food we eat and the nourishment it brings, so scripture is a source of food and nourishment too. It is God feeding us with his word. Then there is that marvelous passage in Isaiah 55:10–12:

> For as the rain and the snow come down from heaven,
> and do not return there until they have watered
> the earth,
> making it bring forth and sprout,
> giving seed to the sower and bread to the eater,
> so shall my word be that goes out from my mouth;
> it shall not return to me empty,
> but it shall accomplish that which I purpose,
> and succeed in the thing for which I sent it.

God's word is truly efficacious. It works, because the one who speaks the word works. God's word creates and redeems, fulfilling God's purposes. For Christians the power of the scriptures comes wonderfully in conjunction with the Eucharist in this story about the two companions traveling from Jerusalem to Emmaus in Luke 24. There, we are told, as the word of God was broken open by the Word of God on the road, Cleopas and his companion recognized the Word as their hearts were burning within them (v. 32).

Furthermore, as Jesus the Word dined with them, they knew him in the breaking of the bread—taking, blessing, breaking, and giving bread, the fourfold action of the Eucharist (v. 35). These layers of meaning about scripture within scripture lie behind the fine emphases of George Herbert's poems. That is one of the reasons surely why Herbert, in considering the education of a priest, has this to say in his pastoral manual *The Country Parson*: "The Country Parson is full of all knowledge...but the chief and top of his knowledge consists in the book of books, the storehouse and magazine of life and comfort, the Holy Scriptures. There he sucks and lives."

The Presence of Christ

The Liturgy of the Word is meant to celebrate the presence of Christ, who is the Word proclaimed. In fact, as our official liturgical documents make clear, Christ is present in the assembly of the faithful, in the person of the minister, in the word and in the eucharistic species par excellence. The Constitution on the Sacred Liturgy from Vatican II affirms, "Christ is always present in His Church, especially in her liturgical celebrations. He is present in the sacrifice of the Mass, not only in the person of His minister...but especially under the Eucharistic species....He is present in His word, since it is He Himself who speaks when the holy scriptures are read in the Church. He is present, lastly, when the Church prays and sings...."[5]

And the Constitution on Divine Revelation states, "The Church has always venerated the divine Scriptures just as she venerates the body of the Lord, since, especially in the sacred liturgy, she unceasingly receives and offers to the faithful the bread of life from the table both of God's word and of Christ's body."[6] The entire Christian tradition is marked by an awareness of the modes of Christ's presence.

If we turn to chapter 1 of the "Decree on the Most Holy Sacrament of the Eucharist" from the Council of Trent in 1551, we find this statement:

In the first place the holy Council teaches and openly and without qualification professes that, after the consecration of the bread and wine, our Lord Jesus Christ, true God and true man, is truly, really and substantially contained in the propitious sacrament of the holy Eucharist under the appearances of those things which are perceptible to the senses....[Christ] is nevertheless sacramentally present to us by his substance in many other places in a mode of existing which, though we can hardly express it in words, we can grasp with minds enlightened by faith as possible to God and must most firmly believe.[7]

The council fathers at Trent are clearly aware that the presence of Christ is not to be restricted to the eucharistic gifts. "[He] is sacramentally present to us...*in many other places*...." Indeed, one would have to affirm that nowhere is Christ absent, even though in the church we experience his presence most intensely and really in the Eucharist.

That unparalleled intensity of Christ in the Eucharist is one of the great hallmarks of Catholicism. There is, if you will, an instinctive "feel" for the eucharistic presence among Catholics. Vatican II is, however, calling and inviting us to a more traditional appreciation of Christ's presence, and especially in the scriptures. The Irish systematic and liturgical theologian Raymond Moloney, SJ, wisely comments, "We have been reared to such a reverence for the Lord's unique presence in his sacrament that we often fail to do justice to the other modes of his presence, and in particular to his presence in his Word. If we are not careful, the Liturgy of the Word can appear as simply someone reading a book at you...."[8] This is an area of theology and catechesis in which we still have much work to do. Moloney goes on to point out:

While we insist that there are several ways in which God is really present to his people, there is no rivalry between the various forms of presence. The whole point is that each kind of presence helps the other: God present in the universe, Christ present in our neighbour, the Spirit present within us; and in the middle of all these manifestations of the divine presence stands the Eucharist. It is the sacrament of presence, the center of all the other kinds of presence, and the source of our response to each of them. Our devotion to Christ's Eucharistic presence should make us more aware of and responsive to all these different ways in which Christ is really present to his people.[9]

There is no competition between these various modes of Christ's real presence. They are all so many complementary means provided by God to draw us into his own life, centered in the eucharistic gifts.

One of the many ways in which as a church we may develop this extraordinarily rich scriptural-eucharistic perspective is through preaching. So many opportunities for this emerge in the course of preaching on the scriptures, and so it is to this issue of preaching that we now turn, and here again we shall find inspiration in the work of George Herbert.

4

Preachers on Preaching: Alan of Lille, George Herbert, William Barclay

The act of preaching has a sacramental quality, in the sense that and to the extent that it is about transformation....When I preach, what I ought to be doing is witnessing to conversion in myself, and in others....Transformation has occurred, is occurring and will occur. And, therefore, I not only preach for conversion, I preach from conversion....The more deeply I am converted, the more hungry I become, the more deeply I realize my unconversion....It's a cliché, I suppose, but like many clichés not without truth, that the best sermons are the ones you preach to yourself....We are there at the Eucharist so that we may be changed into his likeness, from glory to glory. We are there not to change certain things in the world, which we then adore from a distance. We are there so that the transubstantiation may occur in us. So the sermon, as a moment in the eucharistic transaction, is precisely bound up with the changes that are going on, and will go on, in us, in the whole business of our living in the Body of Christ, and most specifically in our receiving the elements of the Holy Eucharist.

Rowan D. Williams[1]

Part of what it means to be human is the difficult task of listening. Part of what it means to be liturgical and eucharistic is the very difficult task of listening. One of the most challenging things I do as a permanent deacon is the preparation of a homily. Going through the diaconal courses en route to ordination in St. Chad's Cathedral, Birmingham, England, we had a fine but all too brief introduction to homiletics from the late Msgr. James Dunlop Crichton, the well-known popular liturgist.[2] Some twenty-two years later, I have preached many homilies, but preparing a homily still remains difficult. As a teacher of theology, I don't find public speaking, or working with adult faith formation, enormously problematic. Preaching, however, is altogether different. One is trying to reach toward the conversion of mind and heart, including one's own mind and heart. That is the thrust of the chapter's long opening citation on preaching from Archbishop Rowan Williams, a passage that is worth much pondering.

Peter Gomes, the late professor at Harvard Divinity School and a noted preacher, made the following comment in an essay about preaching. Speaking of the omnipopularity of spirituality–self-help books, and he especially notes the *Chicken Soup* variety, Gomes says, "For those of us in the business of trying to make words make sense, this may well seem a threatening situation. Who cares to hear what we may have to say when people are much more interested in trying to articulate that which is within themselves, permitting that inner self and inner voice an authentic and liberating communication?"[3]

Gomes tells us, "Preaching begins with the underrated, homiletical art of listening both to God and to the people of God," and suggests that preaching is a matter of trust in four fundamental ways. First, "Trust yourself. Trust that you have something to say, and that it is worthwhile." Second, "Trust the text." For Gomes, trusting the text throws up some key questions: "What is this text saying? What does it give me permission to say? How have others dealt with this? What did they know that I do not? What do I know that they did not?…Trust that the text not only spoke but speaks." Third, "Trust the people." Gomes continues, "Most congregations will their preachers to succeed for there are better forms of amusement than to watch a preacher die in the pulpit. Most people will listen to you if you listen to them."

Fourth, "Trust God." "Trust that God has a word for you, and that out of your prayer and your study, and out of all your choice of words, that word which is God's word for you and for your people will be heard even if it is not the word you had in mind when you began."[4] These trustful recommendations of Gomes are very solid advice.

As I read and pondered Gomes's essay, I found myself recalling some of the things being said by great preachers of the past. That gives comfort. If preaching the good news of Christ did not seem to have strong lines of continuity down through the ages, it would be strange indeed. Our indwelling in holy scripture, our efforts to bring others through the preaching of the word to the encounter with the God who is the Mystery of Communion should not be an experience alien from one generation to the next. This chapter looks at three great preachers of the past who have offered a toolbox for preachers derived from their own experiences of proclaiming the word: from the medieval period, Alan of Lille; from the Reformation period, George Herbert; and from the modern period, William Barclay. Each endorses, in his own way, what Peter Gomes has to say about preaching.

Alan of Lille (ca. 1128–1202)

There is nothing known of Alan of Lille's early life. Born in Lille, Flanders, he was a student at Paris and Chartres in the 1130s and 1140s, during the teaching time of Peter Abelard, Thierry of Chartres, and Gilbert of Poitiers, and finally he himself became a teacher in Paris. He was one of the last great scholars of Paris before the philosophy of Aristotle became generally available. He ended his days as a Cistercian at Cîteaux. He was a prolific author, "well read and possessed of almost encyclopaedic learning," especially in the field of speculative theology.[5] The *Art of Preaching*, a manual for preachers, is one of his works in practical theology and has been described as "pioneering."[6] The art of preaching in the schools of the day was to become "a highly formal art," satisfying "the scholastic desire for order, exactness, and meticulousness."[7]

Alan is suspicious of anything that might threaten the independence, or better the giftlike character of revelation, and so also of theology. This is especially true for the preacher. He should stay very close to the word of scripture: "Nor in the expounding of his authority, should [the preacher] move too quickly away from his text, in case the beginning should be out of keeping with the middle and the middle with the end." The text of holy scripture was all-important for him. "[He] loved Scripture and the intellectual excitement of discovering fresh ways to use scriptural comparisons and illustrations."[8]

Alan's love of scripture nonetheless did not blind him to the use of other authors, even non-Christian authors. He writes, "[The preacher] may also on occasion insert sayings of the pagan writers—just as the Apostle Paul sometimes introduces quotations from the philosophers into his epistles...." Alan criticizes "a tendency to apply terms taken from natural science to the study of theology, with the result that those scarcely capable of understanding common theatre presume to be able to understand the disputations of angels."[9] Scripture remains supreme for him, and, of course, it is scripture as understood in our previous chapter.

"Preaching," maintains Alan, "is an open and public instruction in faith and behavior, whose purpose is the forming of men...."[10] He calls this "forming of men" "the ultimate reason for preaching." "Preaching is that instruction which is offered to many, in public, and for their edification." Preaching has to do with spiritual matters, about how to live a good life but toward a divine end. This "forming of men" has to do with their being graced, with their divinization. In a sermon for Ash Wednesday, Alan speaks, as one would expect, of the need to turn away from sin. This repentance is central to the "forming of men," but the forming goes much further. He continues in this sermon to say to the sinner turning from sin: "*Deificatus es, et ascendes ad Deum,* You are divinized, and you are ascending to God."[11]

41

Repentance, ongoing conversion is necessary as we are drawn into the divine life.

For this most serious of reasons, then, "preaching should not contain jesting words, or childish remarks.... Such preaching is theatrical and full of buffoonery, and in every way to be condemned." There is no room in his judgment for frivolous jokes. On the contrary, preaching should be substantive, both in language and in content: "There should be some weight in the thought of a good sermon, so that it may move the spirits of its hearers, stir up the mind, and encourage repentance." Being substantive in language does not mean, however, that preaching should be superficially impressive with a register of alien words and speech: "Preaching should not glitter with verbal trappings, with purple patches, nor should it be too much enervated by the use of colorless words: the blessed keep to a middle way." If preaching has to do with this divinizing of people, this "forming of men," these guidelines are very important. They serve to remind the preacher that the sermon cannot be "to win the admiration of man" if it is to contribute effectively to his divinization.

There are three kinds of preaching for Alan: by the spoken word, by the written word, by deed or example. There ought to be a concord and consonance between the preacher's spoken word and moral performance. The preacher "should also assure his listeners that he will speak briefly and to their profit, and that he has been led to speak only by his love for his listeners; that he does not speak as one greater in knowledge or in wisdom, or as one who lives a better life, but because things are sometimes revealed to the little ones which are not shown to the great...." This idea that the preacher should speak briefly is emphasized further: "Let the sermon be brief, in case prolixity should cause boredom."

George Herbert (1593–1633)

George Herbert, the younger brother of Lord Herbert of Cherbury (who is commonly regarded as the father of deism), was born of an aristocratic family in Montgomeryshire, in the Welsh borders, in 1593. After his studies at the University of Cambridge, Trinity College, Herbert followed what Louis Bouyer calls "worldly ambitions and politics"—he served as a member for Montgomeryshire in the 1624 Parliament—before finally becoming a deacon in 1624.[12]

Herbert married Jane Danvers in 1629, and the following year he was ordained priest in Salisbury Cathedral. He became rector of Bemerton, near Salisbury in the southwest of England. Bouyer sums up the two remaining years of Herbert's short life in these words: "He spent the two remaining years of his life in this rectory, leaving it only for brief excursions to the cathedral town to which his love for choral liturgy and music drew him."[13] Herbert has left us some of the most remarkable poetry in the English language, poetry that, in the words of David F. Ford, "is shot through with sheer delight in God."[14]

Herbert has also left us a very fine manual on the life of the priest, *The Country Parson, His Character and Rule of Life.*[15] There we find a chapter entitled "The Parson Preaching," and it begins with these words: "The Country Parson preaches constantly: the pulpit is his joy and his throne." The pulpit is the parson's *joy*. He enjoys being there; he enjoys breaking open God's word for his congregation.

It is not so much that the parson *finds* joy in preaching as that the Joy that is God finds him. The mention of the pulpit as the parson's "throne" might suggest to us a certain imperialism that could lead to arrogance on the part of the preacher. Not for Herbert. The king sits on the throne, not in his own right, but as placed there by God, by divine right. As the king is God's vicegerent on earth, so the preacher is God's vicegerent in the pulpit. He stands in God's place; indeed, the pulpit is God's place from which God speaks his word. The pulpit-as-throne is the place for obediential listening to the word of God, for the parson-preacher himself as much as for the congregation. This obediential listening makes demands on the hearers, so that Herbert can say, "Sermons are dangerous things....None goes out of the church as he came in, but either better or worse....The

Word of God shall judge us." There is an efficacy to the word of God that makes a difference when it is spoken in scripture and sermon: "None goes out of the church as he came in."

The efficacy of the preached word is to no small extent mediated by the preacher. The word of God judges the quality of work on the preacher's part as well as the quality of reception on the congregation's part. To aid the quality of preparation Herbert offers advice to the preacher. The advice offered is twofold. First, it has to do with the pragmatics of preaching, knowing the craft of preaching. This is how Herbert puts it: "When he preaches, he procures attention by all possible art...both by earnestness of speech (it being natural to men to think that where there is much earnestness there is somewhat worth hearing)...."

Herbert would be appalled at what is sometimes the banal speech of the street that too easily can find its way into the pulpit. Speech in the pulpit should be earnest, serious, designed to make an impact, not produce mirth and merriment. This, of course, does not mean that there is no room for humor in the pulpit, but rather that humor is conveyed with great care and discernment. As well as seriousness of speech, the preacher should also know his congregation well and accommodate his speech to the congregation. This is how he puts it: "By a diligent and busy cast of eye on his auditors, [he lets] them know that he observes who marks and who does not...." Eye contact with the congregation, "a diligent and busy cast of eye," alerts the preacher to those who are feeling compelled to pay attention and who are not, and to fine-tune what he is saying so that attention is maximally engaged.

In some respects, Herbert becomes a little condescending, as when he says,

> Sometimes he tells them stories and sayings of others, according as his text invites him; for them also men heed and remember better than exhortations, which though earnest, yet often die with the sermon, especially with country people, which are thick and heavy, and hard to

raise to a point of zeal and fervency, and need a mountain of fire to kindle them; but with stories and sayings
they will remember.

In contrast with the refined theological educators at the University
of Cambridge, country people may have seemed to him "thick and
heavy, and hard to raise to a point of zeal and fervency." Despite
the obvious condescension, however, the remark is made in order
to make the preacher aware of his responsibility to kindle a fire
under the "thick and heavy." In other words, he is not content with
pointing the finger at the congregation for not being on fire with
the word of God. He recognizes his responsibility to light that fire.

For Herbert the lighting of fire in preaching sparks from holiness of life: "By these and other means the parson procures attention; but the character of his sermon is holiness: he is not witty, or
learned, or eloquent but holy." Herbert is quite specific about how
holiness is gained and maintained in preaching, and he offers five
rules. First, by carefully choosing among the texts of the scriptures.
Herbert's preaching is not lectionary based and situated, and the
preacher must choose carefully. Had he the lectionary to go by,
Herbert's point still would stand. Choose carefully from the texts
appointed in the lectionary. How does one choose a particular scriptural text from the appointed readings? This takes us to his second
rule: "By dipping and seasoning all our words and sentences in our
hearts before they come into our mouths…so that the auditors may
plainly perceive that every word is heart-deep." For the words of
scripture articulated in the homily to be "heart-deep" they must have
found a home in the preacher's heart. The preacher must linger long
with the scriptures so that his preaching is "utterance" and not "outerance." Utterance is the word reflected and pondered; outerance is
failing to choose carefully the words with which to reach the heart.
Third, the preacher should turn to God in spontaneous prayer during preaching. Herbert intended this to be done aloud, as was the
custom of the day. But there is nothing to prevent such spontaneous
prayer today, even if it is not done aloud. Prayer during preaching

leads the preacher to recognize this is God's work, not human work: "Oh my Master, on whose errand I come, let me hold my peace, and do thou speak thyself, for thou art Love, and when thou teachest all are scholars." Fourth are "frequent wishes of the people's good." This is Jacobean English for what we might describe as "loving the people." The preacher needs not only to love the people. The people need to know that they are loved by him. They need to hear and feel his love for them. Herbert cites the Second Letter of St. Paul to the Corinthians as a paradigm in this respect. This is what he says: "How full of affections! [St. Paul] joys and he is sorry, he grieves and he glories: never was there such care of a flock expressed, safe in the great shepherd of the fold, who first shed tears over Jerusalem, and afterwards blood." Fifth, "by an often urging of the presence and majesty of God." Herbert is saturated with God's presence, with a profound sense that in God we live and move and have our being. Recognizing God as very present gives to the preacher, along with the other four rules, a permeative sense of holiness, a holiness that is caught by the congregation.

If all these helps and hints and words about the art of preaching seem too prosaic, let us finally turn to Herbert's poem, "The Windows," for their most pleasing representation:[16]

Lord, how can a man preach thy eternal Word?
    He is a brittle, crazy glass:
Yet in thy temple thou dost afford
    This glorious and transcendent place,
    To be a window, through thy grace.

But when thou dost anneal in glass thy story,
    Making thy life to shine within
The holy Preacher's; then the light and glory
    More rev'rend grows, and more doth win:
    Which else shows watrish, bleak and thin.

Doctrine and life, colours and light, in one
    When they combine and mingle, bring

> A strong regard and awe: but speech alone
>   Doth vanish like a flaring thing,
>   And in the ear, not conscience ring.

It is the incarnation of Christ in the preacher, "making thy life to shine within / the holy Preacher's," conforming the preacher to Christ whose representative he is, that makes the preacher, who is by nature "a brittle, crazy glass," a "window" into grace. What a magnificent theology of preaching!

William Barclay (1907–1978)

When I was a teenager and later an undergraduate, William Barclay was a name in Scotland to be reckoned with. He was a professor of New Testament at the University of Glasgow, a Presbyterian minister, and a household name because of his frequent preaching appearances on television. So, it came as a surprise to me to read these words of his: "The ministry involves preaching, and all my life I have regarded preaching with dread....For me to enter a pulpit has always been a literally terrifying experience."[17] He was so nervous before getting into the pulpit that he continually needed company. Barclay preached for more than forty-five years, and in his spiritual autobiography he offers us some hard-won conclusions about preaching, in fact, eleven conclusions.[18]

First, "a great deal of the effect of preaching depends on technique."[19] Barclay realizes that *technique* is not a word that spiritually minded people probably find attractive with respect to preaching, but he draws an analogy between the art of preaching and the art of cooking. Two cooks can use the same ingredients, follow the same basic recipe, yet one produces an attractive meal and the other an uneatable mess. So with preachers. "One will rivet the attention and another will produce sleep." Barclay concludes, "Let no budding preacher ever despise teaching on how to preach."

Second, "preaching must be by compulsion....The preacher is the man who speaks because he cannot keep silent." The good news that is the gospel of our Lord Jesus Christ has taken root in his heart and compels him to speak. It is what St. Paul meant when he said to the Corinthians: "Woe to me if I do not proclaim the gospel!" (1 Cor 9:16).

Third, "preaching must be by conviction." Conviction is not something that can be simulated. When a preacher believes intensely in what he is saying, it comes through, even if those who hear him think he may be misguided or downright wrong. Preaching by conviction gives the definite impression that "something tremendous is at stake." "The plain fact is that unless the preacher can give the impression that what he is talking about matters to himself, he will certainly not make it matter to anyone else."

Fourth, "preaching must be derived from experience." This is not to affirm that one's own experience is the norm for all and for every experience. Rather, what Barclay is getting at is that without the deep, personal experience that comes from lingering long both in the Lord's presence and in the tradition, one will be but echoing what others have said, and to some extent it will have a hollow sound.

Fifth, preaching ought to be "biblically and credally centered." Coming from the Reformation tradition, one expects Barclay to propose a scripture-centered preaching, but credally? By *credally* he means the church's belief, or, as a Catholic might put it, the church's tradition. Preaching is not free thinking, but an attempt to unpack the word of God. People are more informed than ever, and what they want from the preacher is "the only expertise that he possesses," that is, his skill "in the interpretation of the Bible and of the Christian faith."

Sixth, preaching should be systematic. As a Presbyterian in the 1950s, '60s, and early '70s, Barclay's preaching was not focused on the lectionary but on the scriptures as such. His complaint here is that a preacher could, by choosing certain particular and favorite passages, set up his own canon of scripture within the canon of scripture. "Systematic preaching will bring the congregation face-to-face with the whole of Scripture, and it will have the not unimportant advantage that the preacher will have his subject prescribed for him in advance, and there will be no last-minute search for something to preach about." What Barclay advocates in "systematic preaching" is what we have now in the three-year lectionary.

Seventh, preaching should also be teaching. Preaching should not be reduced to exhortation. "There is no point in exhorting people to be Christians until they know what being a Christian means." It is often said in contemporary homiletics that preaching should not be teaching. What is of importance in the statement is that the homily is not a theological lecture. All carefully chosen words in exchange with another are necessarily formational, and formation is teaching. Teaching-in-preaching is not obviously didactic in the sense that one attempts on Trinity Sunday to lay out St. Thomas Aquinas's psychological analogy for the Trinity. Avoiding such complexities in preaching, however, does not mean falling back on and remaining content with vapid content.

Eighth, to be effective, preaching must also be "a learning ministry." In Barclay's words, "No man can continue to give out, unless he also takes in." In seminary or divinity school a student learned. "All through the days of his ministry he must continue to learn." Barclay tells the story of visiting a secondhand bookshop in Glasgow one day after the final exams in the Divinity Faculty at the end of the academic year. He found the theology shelves very well stocked indeed. As he took down the most current textbooks he found his students had owned them but sold them at the end of the year. Recently I found in the secondhand sale section of our library a copy of the English edition of Kurt Aland's *Synopsis of the Four Gospels*. The student had given this away, but surely there are few books more useful to a student of preaching than a synopsis of the Gospels! Barclay concludes this part of this treatment with the conclusion: "It was as if to say that farewell to college meant farewell to study....I do not envy the congregation which has to sit under the man who has decided that he is released from learning the moment his college door shuts behind him, or who has nervously decided that he will seek the safety of the old orthodoxies and old conventional language." Needless to say, this does not mean that one parades one's learning before one's captive congregation on a Sunday, that one sets out to impress. It simply means that if one is not continuing to learn, then one will have nothing to say in the pulpit.

Ninth, "one of the main aims of preaching must be intelligibility." While in personal study one can go back to a difficult or an opaque passage time and again, wrestle with its meaning, no member of our congregations can do that with the homily. The ordinary person does not speak, nor is she acquainted with the technical language of theology. The profound truths of Christianity must be communicated in ways that are intelligible, and the preacher must continually aim at that. "The preacher cannot assume intelligibility; he must battle for it."

Tenth, preaching must be relevant. People need to be persuaded of the importance of Christian faith and truth to their lives. That is what is intended by relevance. "Relevance" consists in the recognition that the preacher is speaking to the actual lives of people. In Barclay's words: "At least once in a while every person in the congregation should be able to say of something in a service: 'That means me!'"

Eleventh is sincerity, sheer honesty. "There are many accents which a man may counterfeit," says Barclay, "but the one accent he cannot counterfeit is the accent of sincerity....Nothing can be a substitute for the accent of honesty."

Conclusion

Professor Peter Gomes notes that "the single most requested short courses in continuing education among the clergy, both in school and at professional conferences, are courses in preaching."[20] I am unsure whether this claim of Gomes is accurate or not, but I am certain that any attempt to renew our preaching tradition and to hone our preaching skills can only be advantaged by turning to the past great masters of preaching, of whom Alan of Lille, George Herbert, and William Barclay are but three.

5

The Eucharist: Through the Lens of the *Catechism*

The Eucharist makes the Church.

Catechism of the Catholic Church, par. 1396

The Eucharist, Source and Summit of Ecclesial Life

This chapter provides a summary of Catholic eucharistic theology by attending to the clear and carefully crafted synthesis provided in the *Catechism of the Catholic Church*. The relevant section on the Eucharist in the *Catechism* opens with these words: "The holy Eucharist completes Christian initiation. Those who have been raised to the dignity of the royal priesthood by baptism, configured more deeply to Christ by confirmation, participate with the whole community in the Lord's own sacrifice by means of the Eucharist" (par. 1322). This sets the tone for the entire treatment of the Eucharist. It is understood in a truly ecclesial way: it brings Christian initiation to term, the royal priesthood of all believers is affirmed, and the entire church participates in the unique sacrifice of the Lord on Calvary, represented here, a topic to which we return when reflecting on the Eucharist as theodicy. Citing from Vatican II's *Decree on Priests*, the *Catechism* emphasizes the centrality of the Eucharist in an unmistakable and clear fashion: "The other sacraments, and indeed all ecclesiastical ministries and works of the apostolate, are bound up with the

Eucharist and are oriented toward it" (1324). This is because the Eucharist is the central mechanism, as it were, of God's divinizing us, drawing us into participation and sharing in the trinitarian life (1325), and because in this action/event we are united with the heavenly liturgy and anticipate the Parousia (1326). These initial paragraphs of the *Catechism* are beautiful and very traditional in emphasis. They affirm what Aquinas, for example, said in the thirteenth century: that the Eucharist is the consummation and goal of all the sacraments.[1]

What Is This Sacrament Called?

The Eucharist is referred to by different names, and in fact, the *Catechism* includes some sixteen different names for the rite. How we name the Eucharist is significant because "often it helps us to locate our understanding in particular historical circumstances."[2] Thus, for example, the Orthodox churches regularly term the celebration the *Synaxis* or the Holy and Divine Liturgy, while Reformation traditions seem to prefer the Lord's Supper or the Holy Communion.

The origins of the Eucharist are probably to be found in our Lord's adaptation of the Jewish rite of grace before and after meals. Raymond Moloney, a lifelong scholar of the Eucharist, describes this rite: "Grace before meals was a ritual of blessing God over bread and then sharing the bread among those present. Grace after meals was a similar ritual but with wine."[3] What our Lord did was to celebrate this ordinary ritual of grace before and after meals in a new way, relating its meaning to his act of worship on the cross. In the early days of the apostolic tradition, it is very probable that the Eucharist was celebrated before and after a community meal, the whole phenomenon being known as "the breaking of the bread." Then, as ecclesial understanding began to develop, the meal was dropped and the two rituals became fused into one great prayer of blessing and thanksgiving. This was to become in later terminology the eucharistic prayer, or the anaphora.

The Eucharist in the Economy of Salvation

Paragraphs 1333–44 of the *Catechism* bring together the story of the Eucharist from its Old Testament foreshadowings in the exodus and Passover to the institution of the Eucharist at the Last Supper. "By celebrating the Last Supper with his apostles in the course of the Passover meal, Jesus gave the Jewish Passover its definitive meaning" (1340). This is an assumption on the part of the *Catechism*. There is a chronological discrepancy in the Gospel accounts of this last meal of the Lord. The Synoptics all take it to be a Passover meal, but St. John has the Passover meal being celebrated on the evening of the Lord's death. The discrepancy, on the basis of the New Testament evidence, is strictly speaking, insoluble.[4] Undoubtedly, however, it is a very short step from a meal with Passover connotations—since it was celebrated during that last week of Jesus' life, a week in which the Passover was celebrated—to a Passover meal. Moloney points out that one cannot press the notion of the Eucharist as a Christian Passover meal too far for at least two reasons. First, "the Eucharist was not instituted on the elements proper to the Passover," such elements as lamb, bitter herbs, and in the early centuries, unleavened bread. Second, the Passover was celebrated only once a year, whereas the Eucharist was a regular and frequent celebration. Moloney's conclusion seems to follow logically and theologically: "Even if the Last Supper were a Passover, the Eucharist was established on elements common to any Jewish festive meal, whether Passover or not."[5] This chronological conundrum is not a huge theological issue, but it is good to be aware of it.

The Liturgical Celebration of the Eucharist

The *Catechism* rightly affirms that the "fundamental structure" of the Eucharist is the Liturgy of the Word, followed by the Liturgy of the Eucharist. Moloney helpfully comments, "Each of these sanctions has a separate origin in customs with which our

Lord was familiar. The Liturgy of the Word comes out of the synagogue service in which our Lord participated every Sabbath (Luke 4:16). The Liturgy of the Eucharist…comes out of the table rituals with which every Jew was familiar from childhood on."[6] At some time in the earliest church, for which we do not now have the precise data, these two rituals of Word and Eucharist were brought together in what we now call the Mass. The *Catechism* then goes on to provide us with that magnificent earliest description of the Mass that we possess from outside the New Testament in paragraph 1345, from Justin Martyr's *First Apology* (par. 65–67). Indeed, it comes back to Justin's celebrated description a number of times.

In this central, liturgical celebration "the Eucharistic table set for us is the table both of the word of God and of the body of the Lord" (1346), retrieving for us the same movement of Luke 24 when the Lord is known both in his explanation of the scriptures and in the breaking of the bread (1347). The *Catechism* sets before us the sequence of the *lex orandi*, the law of prayer. The complex celebration of the Eucharist is made up of various parts. First, the gathering, in which Christ, "the principal agent of the Eucharist," represented in the person of the bishop or priest, summons the people for celebration (1348). It is then followed by the Liturgy of the Word, the readings from scripture, the homily, and the general intercessions. The presentation of the offerings now takes place, and here too the *Catechism* turns to St. Justin to provide both a description and a rationale (1351).

The eucharistic prayer is "the heart and summit of the celebration" (1352) and is made up of the following parts: the preface (giving thanks to the Father, in Christ through the Holy Spirit); the epiclesis, the invocation of the Holy Spirit to transform the bread and the wine so that those who receive the gifts may themselves be transformed; the institution narrative; the anamnesis, recalling the great saving works of God in the past, culminating with the Paschal Mystery of the Lord. Msgr. Robert Sokolowski of Catholic University shows how, as we move into the eucharistic prayer, into the institution narrative, the language changes and establishes the christological-ministerial axis of the prayer:

> In a sacramentally and grammatically perceptible way, Christ becomes the speaker of the words of institution and the doer of the gestures associated with them. Through quotation, the words and gestures of institution become those of Christ, as the "we" of the community, the body of Christ, becomes the "I" of Christ, the head of his body, the church. In this assumption of the words and gestures of the priest, Christ becomes not only the one offered, but also the one who offers the sacrifice of the Mass.[7]

The very words speak and breathe an ordered church, yet an ordered church in which all are with Christ the *totus Christus*, the whole Christ, head and members, but differently. Toward the end of the eucharistic prayer, the intercessions now occur in which the church formally acknowledges her communion with the whole church of heaven and earth. Finally comes the rite of communion, and here yet again, St. Justin is cited at some length (1355).

Now the *Catechism* proceeds to the *lex credendi*, the law of belief, the meaning of the eucharistic celebration. It is summarized as thanksgiving, memorial, and presence. Aidan Nichols nicely draws our attention to the trinitarian shape of the section on eucharistic doctrine. Just as the Trinity is Father, Son, and Holy Spirit, so the *Catechism* speaks paterologically (to the Father), christologically (in Christ), and pneumatologically (through the Holy Spirit).[8] Nichols's language is a bit cumbersome, but it has the merit of underscoring in a very clear way the trinitarian shape.

Paterological Thanksgiving

Thanksgiving is addressed principally to the Father. Noting that the very word *Eucharist* means in Greek "thanksgiving," the *Catechism* affirms that the Eucharist is "a sacrifice of praise and thanksgiving for the work of creation. In the Eucharistic sacrifice the whole of creation loved by God is presented to the Father through the death and the resurrection of Christ" (1359). Through it "the church sings the glory of God in the name of all creation" (1361). The Eucharist as the sacrifice of praise is *to* the Father, but *through* and *with* and *in* Christ.

Christological Memorial

"The Eucharist is the memorial of Christ's Passover, making present the sacramental offering of his unique sacrifice in the liturgy of the church which is his body" (1362). The Greek word for memorial is *anamnesis*. In the memorial of the Eucharist is found the integral unity of the unique, once-for-all sacrifice of Christ on the cross with this present celebration. "The Eucharist…re-presents (makes present) the sacrifice of the cross" (1366), so that "the sacrifice of Christ and the sacrifice of the Eucharist are *one single sacrifice*" (1367). Because there is no Christ without the church, Christ as the head of his Body the Church, "the church participates in the offering of her head" so that "the Eucharist is also the sacrifice of the Church" (1368). In practical terms, this means that the entire lives of the faithful, in all their multifaceted complexity, are united to and associated with this sacrifice of Christ-Church: "The lives of the faithful, their praise, sufferings, prayer, and work, are united with those of Christ and with his total offering, and so acquire a new value" (1368). Catholics do not have a theological theodicy in the face of illness and pain and suffering. Rather, in their ongoing participation in the Eucharist they *perform* a theodicy through union/communion with Christ their head in his sacrificial movement. Illness, suffering, and pain are conjoined and co-offered with the Christ in whom they live and move and have their being. We return to this in chapter 8, "The Eucharist as Theodicy."

With this perspective, we recognize that the Eucharist is not only offered for the church, but also by the church, by the whole church, and with the people of the church acting in different ways, according to their orders/*ordines*, "with the priest alone acting in the person of Christ the head, and he alone consecrating the gifts."[9] This ecclesial sense of the eucharistic sacrifice includes all those who have gone before us marked with the sign of faith. "To the offering of Christ are united not only the members still here on earth, but also those already in *the glory of heaven*" (1370). This includes those faithful departed who "have died in Christ but are not yet wholly purified," who are being purged as they prepare to move into the light and peace of Christ (1371). Purgatory is an area of the Eucharist and of Catholic doctrine about which more needs to be said. For many Catholics, the doctrine of Purgatory is not especially center stage, and yet it is a very obviously necessary doctrine. If God is "the Love that will not let us go"—paraphrasing the famous hymn of the blind nineteenth-century Scottish Presbyterian hymn writer and theologian George Matheson—and if we genuinely recognize our permeative unloveliness, and if through death those who are unlovely move into the presence of the one who is Love, the encounter demands the final hearing of unloveliness by Love. That is Purgatory, and we shall see something more of it when we come to John Henry Newman's epic poem "The Dream of Gerontius."

Pneumatological Presence

Referring to presence as "pneumatological," which means "to do with the Holy Spirit," may initially seem strange, especially to Western Catholics. The *Catechism* emphasizes that the eucharistic presence comes about "in the efficacy of the word of Christ and *of the action of the Holy Spirit*" (1375). There is a very clear pneumatological emphasis here. Christ is present in many ways to his church, as we have already noted: in his word, in the church's prayer, in the poor, the sick and imprisoned, in the sacraments, in the sacrifice of the Mass, in the person of his minister, and "he is present...most *especially in the Eucharistic species*" (1373). The church judges the mode of Christ's presence under the eucharistic species as unique because, while these other modes of Christ's presence are very real indeed, the presence of Christ in the eucharistic species "is presence in the fullest sense.…It is a substantial presence" (1374).

The eucharistic presence comes about through "the efficacy of the word of Christ and of the action of the Holy Spirit." This change from bread and wine to the body and blood of Jesus Christ is "fittingly and properly called transubstantiation" (1376). This presence lasts as long as the sign of this presence lasts, and receives adoration from the faithful (1378–80). To this we return briefly when speaking about the theology of Benediction.

In chapter 3, mention was made of the various modes of Christ's presence. As noted, talk about different modes of Christ's presence, or the manifold presence of Christ, has been difficult for some Catholics. Some feel that this kind of language detracts from the presence of Christ in the eucharistic gifts themselves. The fear is not altogether ill founded. One could say without contradiction, I think, that there has been some lessening of appreciation for and reverence of the eucharistic gifts in the posture, disposition, and knowledge of the faithful. This is unfortunate, but to counter it does not mean retreating from the teaching of the church on the modes of Christ's presence in order to emphasize only the eucharistic gifts, but rather to receive more fully that teaching. Moloney, whom we have cited before in this respect, is quite outstanding in his commentary:

> Christ's presence to his church is the presupposition of any liturgical celebration, so that any particular mode of his presence within that context comes about not in order simply to establish a presence, but in order to deepen our response to a presence already there. Consequently, the change that takes place in the Eucharistic gifts does not come about as though the problem to be overcome were still one of spatial distance. The real problem is one of what we might call moral distance, namely one of our lack of response. He comes close to us under the species of bread and wine primarily in order to deepen our

response to this and to the other modes of his presence by drawing us into an altogether special union with himself through holy Communion. He then continues his presence among us in the tabernacle in order to keep that union alive in our hearts from Mass to Mass and from Communion to Communion.[10]

There is remarkable balance and fine eucharistic theology in this paragraph, which offers opportunity for meditative appropriation. This is the kind of paragraph that is only possible after many years of thinking about and teaching the Eucharist. In practical terms, there is no rivalry, as it were, between the various modes of presence. How could there be? "At the center of them all there is Christ's presence in host and cup which, as the sacrament of presence *par excellence*, helps to maintain all the others and keeps us sensitive to them."[11]

Other Aspects of the Eucharist

The Eucharist "is wholly directed toward the intimate union of the faithful with Christ through Communion" (1382). The faithful should prepare themselves carefully to receive the Eucharist (1385–87). The *Catechism* posits five major fruits of holy communion (1391–98):

1. It augments our union with Christ.
2. It separates us from sin and strengthens us against it.
3. The Eucharist makes the Church.
4. Through it we are committed more to the poor.
5. It makes urgent our desire for the unity of Christians.

The Eucharist: "Pledge of the Glory to Come"

As we live and celebrate the Eucharist, we anticipate in hope the Parousia of the Lord. "There is no surer pledge or clearer sign of this great hope in the new heavens and the new earth 'in which righteousness dwells,' than the Eucharist" (1405). At the Parousia, the human invitation into the life of the Blessed Trinity will be creaturely complete, but that invitation to communion is already in place here and now in the Eucharist. As Moloney puts it, "Eternal life will be our Communion with [the Trinity] forever, but this Communion is already a reality for us in the Communion which we celebrate in every Mass."[12]

Conclusion

This summary of eucharistic theology provided by the *Catechism of the Catholic Church* is both very rich and very straightforward. It bears careful study and attention. In the next two chapters we pick up elements of eucharistic theology noted here and try to address them more substantially: the Eucharist and theodicy (the problem of evil and suffering) and the theology of Benediction. We shall also look at the eucharistic theology of an earlier twentieth-century English-language theologian, the Benedictine Anscar Vonier, in order to see both continuities and developments in our Catholic understanding of the sacrament.

6

Eucharistic Theology: The Sacramental Vision of Anscar Vonier, OSB

A classic example of the best twentieth century eucharistic theology might be the little book, A Key to the Doctrine of the Eucharist *by the Benedictine Anscar Vonier, Abbot of Buckfast, which first saw the light of day in 1925.*

Aidan Nichols, OP[1]

Anscar Vonier was born Martin Vonier in Germany in 1875 and died in 1938 at Buckfast Abbey, England, which he had entered as a novice in 1893. Dom Anscar was ordained in 1898, and after ordination he was sent for doctoral studies to Sant' Anselmo in Rome. He completed his PhD thesis—the title was "De Infinito"—in philosophy in one year and returned to Buckfast Abbey in 1900. His interests were not confined to philosophy. It is recorded that he had a strong interest in scripture—"The Hebrew Bible was always on his desk"—and he was steeped in the Pauline letters.[2]

From 1905 to 1906 Dom Anscar was back to Sant' Anselmo as professor of philosophy, but his life was to change in 1906. On the way to Argentina from Spain with his abbot for the canonical visitation of the Argentinean monastery in Nino Dios, the ship in which they were traveling was wrecked off Cartagena, and Abbot Boniface Natter, having given his lifebelt to another passenger, was among the many who perished. In fact, when the ship broke apart, Vonier stood on one half and watched his abbot drown on the other. Vonier was rescued and, some six weeks later, was elected the second abbot of Buckfast. Convinced that providence had spared him for some special task, he set about rebuilding the abbey church on its ancient, twelfth-century Cistercian foundations. Abbot Wilfrid Upson, OSB, of Prinknash puts into words what Dom Anscar set out to achieve in the rebuilding of the abbey: "His aim was to create something which would draw the unthinking crowds of our pleasure-loving people—to build a tower which would *make* men look up—and looking up to realize it was a thing of God which they were admiring."[3] In an almost parallel fashion, he set about retrieving the doctrine of the Eucharist for his contemporaries, rebuilding it, as it were, on its ancient foundations in the theology of St. Thomas Aquinas. He died at his abbey on St. Stephen's Day, 1938. Buckfast Abbey did not have a telephone, and news of Dom Anscar's death reached the outside world through the news broadcast of the BBC.

The Eucharist Is a Sacrament

In 1925 Dom Anscar published *A Key to the Doctrine of the Eucharist*, a book of some 269 pages, described by Dom Ernest Graf as his "most weighty contribution to theological thought."[4] Describing the effects of the early stages of the Liturgical Movement in England, Aidan Nichols, OP, has this to say: "The primarily historical bent of the first great liturgical scholars of the country, such as the antiquarian Edmund Bishop; the somewhat confusing plethora of theories about the eucharistic sacrifice which jostled for space in orthodox divinity, and a distrust of excessive concern with rubrical minutiae all conspired to ensure that the pre-Great War early stirrings of the Liturgical Movement would not have much resonance in English Catholicism at large."[5] Not an enormously hope-filled picture! Yet, in the years following World War II, Nichols goes on to describe Fr. Conrad Pepler, OP, ascribing a happy change in liturgical interests in England to a number of factors, including "the excellence of the theology of the eucharistic sacrifice produced by two influential writers of the inter-war period, Anscar Vonier, abbot of Buckfast, and the French Jesuit Maurice de la Taille...."[6]

So, what did Dom Anscar have to say about the Eucharist? The immediate answer may be had in two evaluative responses to Vonier. The first comes in the outstanding work of the late Anglican systematic theologian Eric L. Mascall: "For Vonier the fundamental fact about the Eucharist is the fact that it is a sacrament; and the fundamental fact about a sacrament is the fact that it is a *sign*, albeit a sign of a very special kind."[7] The second comes from the Irish Dominican systematic theologian Colman O'Neill, who gives recognition to this particular aspect of Dom Anscar's achievement. "It was a revelation for modern theology," he writes, "when Abbot Anscar Vonier…rediscovered the symbolic dimension of the realism of medieval eucharistic theology."[8] Both Mascall and O'Neill, and there are others, point up that in Vonier's time the symbolic or sacramental dimension of eucharistic theology was not prominent. The very words *symbol* and *sign* seemed to invite in the direction of the Reformation, and this suspicion is still present to some extent. Vonier, however, retrieved this line of thought in a fruitful way, no doubt partly because he had an established base and competence in medieval philosophy.

The notion of the Eucharist as sacrament/sign runs like a leitmotif throughout his work. "The sacramental principle is truly my key," says Vonier in the foreword of *A Key to the Doctrine of the Eucharist*.[9] Consistently, he turns to the work of St. Thomas Aquinas, the only major figure with whose theology he engages, for direction and insight. Vonier saw the sacraments as a kind of "middle world" between God and creation. Sacraments are neither the one nor the other, but participate in both the divine reality and the reality of creation. "Sacraments have a mode of their own, a psychology of their own, a grace of their own."[10] In a word, and a traditional word at that, sacraments bring about what they signify. They are effective causes of grace. "The sacraments are signs of God; they are most perfect signs because, says St. Thomas, they contain and they bring about the very thing they signify."[11]

The regularity with which he takes to task a materialist or physicalist view of the sacraments suggests that he viewed this as something of a pastoral or perhaps catechetical problem in his day. Thus, for example, he insists, "We can never insist enough on this aspect of sacramental theology; before all things and above all things we are dealing with signs and symbols, not with things in their own proper nature, in *propria specie.*"[12] A sacrament "brings back the past, is the voice of the present, reveals the future….The death of Christ is its past; supernatural transformation is its present; eternal glory is its future."[13]

Vonier fully realizes what the sacraments and especially the Eucharist achieve for humankind: "Any effort we make in order to cultivate sacramental thoughts will be rewarded with special fruits in our own spiritual life. It will make us into true mystics."[14] This is because the sacraments are not entirely natural nor entirely divine, but the divine transforming the natural through an act of sheer grace. This graceful reality that the sacraments are has "a face turned toward God as well as a face turned towards man."[15]

The Eucharist Is the Central Sacrament

Before speaking of the Eucharist or, indeed, any of the sacraments, it was Vonier's judgment that we should first be clear about the sacramentality of Jesus Christ. "Sacraments are, through their very nature, an extension of the Incarnation, a variant of that mystery expressed in the words: 'And the Word was made flesh and dwelt among us.' Is not the Son of God made man the Sacrament *par excellence,* the invisible made visible?"[16] The very language he uses brings immediately to mind the great book of Edward Schillebeeckx, OP, *Christ the Sacrament.*[17] The resonance with Schillbeeckx is no coincidence. Both Vonier and Schillebeeckx were steeped in the thought of St. Thomas, and talk of Christ the Sacrament is profoundly Thomist.

The Eucharist is the central sacrament of the primal Sacrament that is Jesus Christ. Approvingly, Vonier cites St. Thomas in this respect:

> Having once grasped the profound fact that the Eucharist is a true sacrament, he never lets go of that idea, and he succeeds in giving us a theology of the Eucharist which is a masterpiece of harmonious thought; he places the sacrament of the altar in the center of the whole sacramental system, and he makes all the other sacraments converge towards it....The supreme sacrament is, of course, the blessed Eucharist. St. Thomas calls it simply *Potissimum inter alia sacramenta.* Yet his way of explaining this supremacy of the Eucharist shows clearly how well he understood the whole sacramental system to be one perfect organism, where the seven arteries of life work in unison.[18]

In another passage he changes his metaphor: "The monument [of the Eucharist] is not a pyramid, standing in isolated greatness in the midst of the desert; the monument is the citadel which crowns the city, I mean the sacramental theology, which leads up to it and leads away from it."[19] Though he does not develop his line of thought in this particular fashion, for Vonier the other sacraments might best be considered as eucharistic, that is to say, as finding their fulfillment and center in the Eucharist, as leading up to it and flowing from it.

The Eucharist Is the Sacrament of Christ's Unique Sacrifice

Vonier did not enter into debate with the profusion of theories about the eucharistic sacrifice of his time but rather "wisely goes behind them to an earlier time."[20] Dom John Chapman points out one of the basic problems in articulating the theology of the eucharistic sacrifice: "Theologians have sometimes seemed as though they first laid down what is the essence of sacrifice, and then showed that God had arranged sacrifices and a central Sacrifice which accorded quite properly with their definitions."[21] Vonier will have nothing to do with this.

"If it is a maxim in the history of religious thought that no error ever achieves success except through the amount of truth on which it feeds, at no time was this more evident than when the reformers started preaching the uselessness of the Eucharistic sacrifice. Their success came from the most permanent of Christian truths, the all-sufficiency of the sacrifice of the cross."[22] Scholars and Christian traditions have found in the Hebrew and New Testament notion of "remembrance"/memory the conceptual solution to the post-Reformation polemics about Calvary and the Eucharist. The Eucharist is the "memorial" of Calvary, the representation of the unique sacrifice of Christ on the Cross. Vonier writes, "The sacrifice of the Christian altar and the sacrifice of Calvary are one and the same sacrifice....The sacrifice of Calvary and the sacrifice of the Eucharist are to each other in the relationship of the *exemplum*; one is the replica of the other. One contains what the other contains."[23]

Jesuit systematic theologian Raymond Moloney writes, "I would wish simply to underline the similarity between this discovery between exegetes and liturgists and the main lines of Vonier's theory....The sacramental principle as put forward by Dom Anscar, seems to the present writer to provide the most satisfactory basis for a theological explanation of the unity of the Eucharist and the Cross."[24] His theological-linguistic preference is to speak of "sacrament-sacrifice," or even "sacramental sacrifice," which he thinks is "the best term" to use.[25] He prefers this kind of language in order to eschew any kind of materialism or physicalism in respect of the Eucharist. There is a real difference between the order of nature and the order of sacrament, though the latter is not less real than the former. In defending their eucharistic theology and faith against Protestants, Catholics have sometimes erred in the direction of what Vonier has called "ultra-realism." This evacuates the notion of sacrament altogether and makes the understanding of sacrifice particularly difficult. Oliver Chase Quick, an important Anglican theologian writing on the sacraments two years after Dom Anscar, in 1927, finds the Benedictine's theology of the Eucharist as sacrificial entirely acceptable. After quoting Vonier at considerable length, Quick concludes, "I could accept almost the whole of the above passage [from Vonier] as a forcible statement of the same doctrine of the Eucharistic sacrifice which I have been trying to defend."[26]

Pulling together Vonier's insights, Liam Walsh, OP, concludes, "[Vonier] sees sacramentality as the key not just to the question of sacrifice but also to the question of presence. It is a unifying idea which requires that the ideas of sacrament and sacrifice should interpenetrate rather than go their separate ways."[27] Interpenetration, sacramental sacrifice, sacrificial sacrament—hallmarks of Anscar Vonier's eucharistic theology.

Transubstantiation

The conviction of faith is that in the Eucharist bread and wine are transformed into the Body and Blood of Christ. "How did it happen? The answer is transubstantiation."[28] As a careful follower of St. Thomas, Vonier adheres to transubstantiation totally. "Transubstantiation as being the most simple—nay, even the most beautiful explanation of all we know of the Eucharistic mystery. If it is not the sacrament itself, it is certainly the sweet and gracious mother of the sacrament. In its simplicity it has all the grace and charm of eternal wisdom."[29] Quite an accolade, but one that makes sense for a devotee of St. Thomas. Criticism of substance as a philosophical category was not yet fully under way when Vonier wrote.

Eucharist and Eschatology

In the wake of the Council of Trent and of polemical eucharistic theology between Protestant and Catholic over sacrifice and real
presence, other aspects of eucharistic theology tended not to be
emphasized. One such aspect was the Eucharist as pledge of the
Parousia. It was not absent, indeed, from the deliberations of Trent,
where we read that the Eucharist "is a pledge of future glory and
everlasting happiness."[30] But it certainly was not a regular emphasis
in eucharistic reflection. We find it in Vonier, not greatly developed,
but it is there. Of all the sacraments he rightly points out their eschatological dimension as pledges of future glory: "The sacramental
graces, taken in their most specific aspect, have this characteristic of
being a pledge of the eternal splendors of the life to come."[31] This
too, of course, he received from his master, St. Thomas, but Vonier
has a nice way of putting it in his own words. "The glory for which
the Eucharistic mystery prepares us is something greater than the
Eucharistic mystery itself....Divine as the Eucharist is, life with Christ
in heaven will be something diviner still."[32]

Conclusion

Dom Anscar was a convinced Thomist, following faithfully
the contours of St. Thomas's eucharistic theology in the language
of St. Thomas. Though he does not mention Pope Leo XIII's
encyclical *Aeterni Patris*, which encouraged the study of St.
Thomas Aquinas, undoubtedly this lies tacitly behind Vonier's
work. While there remains a strong appreciation of Thomist philosophy and theology in the post–Vatican II Catholic Church,
there is a range of others also. One thinks, for example, of exis-
tentialist, phenomenological, and process thought, as well as the
various strands of postmodernism. In this pluralist climate the
appeal and satisfaction stemming from St. Thomas's metaphysics
does not command even within the church the immediate assent
that it did formerly. People feel the need to explore other philo-

sophical and theological avenues to unpack their eucharistic faith, avenues that will resonate with contemporary experience, just as Thomism did for the time of Dom Anscar. So, while Vonier's approach to understanding the Eucharist may not commend itself to everyone today, nonetheless his example of using the most suitable and compelling philosophic tools available to give expression to his eucharistic faith demonstrates how "faith seeking understanding" is to be done.

The Catholic Church was not a formal participant in the ecumenical movement in Vonier's time. It is now. One of the great blessings of Vatican II, and one of the great hopes of Blessed John XXIII, followed by Blessed Pope John Paul II, was to promote unity among Christians. Consequent upon the council there has been a range of initiatives aimed at overcoming the doctrinal impediments between Rome and other churches or ecclesial communities. The perspective of Dom Anscar on the Mass as representing the one unique sacrifice of Christ on the cross is now a commonplace in ecumenical theology, even if it is not fully grasped everywhere. The clear Catholic position is that the Eucharist is not a further sacrifice, but the sacramental representation of the historic sacrifice of Calvary. Vonier anticipated this ecumenical gain in 1925.

As he came to the end of his laudatory review, Dom John Chapman gives what seems to me the highest praise to Vonier when he writes, "It seems to me the great merit of this unpretentious book that it tries to smooth out difficulties and to keep to beaten paths; to make views simple rather than complex, broad rather than hair-splitting. I do not think God meant the Christian religion to be so far-fetched and ingenious and tangled as some theologians make out. It was meant for the poor and the meek even more than for the learned."[33] That is no small accomplishment.

Eucharist as Life: The Essence of Being Human

The value of our liturgy depends on the quality of our Christian living....A piece of wafer and a sip of wine do not constitute a meal in any ordinary sense of the word....Life itself is the meal.

Raymond Moloney, SJ[1]

These opening words by liturgical theologian Raymond Moloney help to link us to the material of chapter 2, "Worship and the Catholic Imagination." The verification of authentic Christian liturgy is the transforming effect it has when we leave the space of the ritual. Nowhere is this more important than in the celebration of the central sacrament of the Eucharist, the subject of this chapter. Why do we celebrate the Eucharist? The immediate answer is because Jesus told us to do this "in memory of him." This command of the Lord has been obeyed down through all the generations of Christian faith from the very beginning. The Eucharist is the source and summit of the church's life, as Vatican II taught, because it is an intensification of life used by God to heal our humanness through making us divine.

All this is well known, and is a well-established element in eucharistic catechesis. Perhaps, however, there is more to say. Perhaps we might go on to say that the Eucharist correlates with life as such, that "the Eucharist responds to some of the most fundamental issues and problems facing human beings both as individuals and as communities."[2] This is the expression of Jesuit liturgist John F. Baldovin, and what I hear him saying is that the

Eucharist goes straight to the heart of what it means to be human. Yes, the Eucharist divinizes us in the ways described in the first chapter, but may we not also say that it humanizes us by holding before us, by rehearsing, by performing in ritual and symbolic mode all those fundamental elements of being human. Those fundamental elements of being human, that obtain in every culture and at every time, are assembly, listening and speaking, eating and drinking, dismissal. And the fundamental elements of the Eucharist are assembly, listening and speaking, eating and drinking, dismissal. There is a sort of correlation between life and Eucharist, and it is this correlation that we now examine in a little more detail.

Describing Human Life

The first fundamental element in being human is what we might call "assembly." *Assembly* has to do with people in some measure or degree of relation. The term stands for the necessary element of human relationality. To be human is to be marked by relationality or, as we have it here, "assembly." We are not on or by our own. Our life in this world comes to be through others, literally through their assembly. Our being depends on the assembly of others: of the love-assembly of our parents, and then later on the continued loving support of those who nurture us—the wider family, friends, school, pastors, and so forth—all enabling us to flourish. Although it sounds a little awkward, "to be" is "to be in and through assembly." Theologian George Pattison puts it like this: "We are, it may be said, loved into selfhood....We are not only not islands, we never were....'I' is itself a learned word...."[3] Reflecting on this helps us recognize another necessary aspect of being human, that is to say, everything about us is gift. We are gifted into being and we are gifted in nurture by others. This leads New Testament scholar and theologian William Countryman to spell out something of our giftedness by others:

71

Gift is the principle on which the Creator has based human existence; it is the most pervasive, even if little noticed, reality of our lives. We have life itself by others' gift of procreation, pregnancy and childbirth. We are sustained in life by the good things of nature and by the labour, generosity and society of other human beings. We are educated by the self-giving of our teachers. We are sustained constantly by gifts—love, forgiveness, reconciliation, pleasure. Our whole life is a fabrication of gifts received, and we ourselves contribute our gifts to the life of others.[4]

What a splendid way to put it! My very existence, and indeed everything about me comes from others. I am gift.

The second element is listening. Much of our life is about listening. We listen to the story of who we are, told by others in family and religious tradition, in school, college, and nation. I have come to treasure in this respect a marvelous quotation from the American literary critic and philosopher Kenneth Burke, who offers us a parable of how we are shaped by conversation, and how listening is primary in all of this. This is what he says:

Imagine that you enter a parlor. You come late. When you arrive, others have long preceded you, and they are engaged in a heated discussion, a discussion too heated for them to pause and tell you exactly what it is about. In fact, the discussion had already begun long before any of them got here, so that no one present is qualified to retrace for you all the steps that had gone before. You listen for a while, until you decide that you have caught the tenor of the argument; then you put in your oar. Someone answers; you answer him; another comes to your defense; another aligns himself against you, to either the embarrassment or gratification of your opponent, depending upon the quality of your ally's assistance. However, the discussion is interminable. The hour grows late, you must

depart. And you do depart, with the discussion vigorously
in progress.[5]

Everyone will recognize immediately what Burke is talking about.
Conversation is absolutely essential to human development, but
there is a certain primacy to listening. Before we can speak at all we
have to hear others sounding out words for our imitation and later
for our comprehension. There is no speaking without listening.

That brings us to the third element in what it means to be
human: speaking. Having listened and thus learned how to speak
we continue to develop our fluency throughout the cycle of life.
Speech is always and necessarily regulated. It is governed by grammar and syntax. There is really no such thing as a private language.
In other words, speaking of its very nature is conversational or, we
might say, dialogical. Speech is words between one and another or
others. But, of course, it is intrinsically connected to the primacy of
listening. One may not be without the other. This is conversation.
This is dialogue, and it is enormously difficult. The Dominican
theologian Timothy Radcliffe says of dialogue: "Dialogue is fruitful when it is the struggle to learn from each other....It is easy to
identify another's errors. Do we have the courage to hear what they
may teach us? The struggle of true dialogue is like Jacob wrestling
with the angel, leaving one wounded and blessed. This demands
of us vulnerability."[6] There's the rub! Real conversation, real dialogue renders us vulnerable, and vulnerability is uncomfortable.
Yet, if we are to advance in wisdom and human communion, vulnerability in conversation is ineluctable.

The next elements are eating and drinking, so obviously basic
to human life. Unless we eat and drink regularly, we grow weak
and die. Yet, these elements—eating and drinking—are more than
the satisfaction of hunger and thirst. The food we eat meets many
hungers, not least the hunger for companionship, a word that
means in Latin "eating bread together." Companionship is sacred.
Companionship in eating and drinking brings a self-evident rich-
ness and depth to these very basic physical and biological activi-

ties. Jeremy Driscoll, OSB, writes, "We produce our food together, we consume it together, we share it with one another. It is an expression of love and desire. It aims at communion....With food we tell one another that we love one another, that we depend upon one another, that we desire the other to live and be well."[7] The nourishment afforded by companionship in communion, a more intense form of what was earlier described as assembly, transforms the physicality of eating and drinking.

Finally, there is the element of dismissal in human life. Our life in this world comes to an end. There are many endings before *the* end, in each of which we have an experience of being sent out, dis-missed. We are dismissed from the womb at birth. In a sense we are dismissed from the family when we go to school. When we take a step beyond school, when we graduate, we are dismissed into the wider complexity of socioeconomic-political life. Dismissal is a continual part of living. Then finally, when we are stripped of everything, we die. The experience of this final dis-missal is anticipated to some extent in all the earlier experiences of dismissal.

Describing Eucharist

The description of the Eucharist that follows shows a certain correlation with the fundamental elements of what it means to be human. In the first place is assembly. There is no Eucharist without an assembly. "Whatever else the Church is, it is the assembly of God's people who have been called to gather as one in the name of Jesus the Lord."[8] The celebration of the Eucharist is never private. The celebration ultimately includes all of God's creation, but especially God's human creatures, and especially those human creatures who are church. In this assembly is hidden the whole church, of all centuries, of all time, and, since the church is for the world, says Jeremy Driscoll, OSB, "in that Church is gathered the whole creation and the desires of every human heart....The meaning of the whole creation and the whole of human history is contained here in ritual form and in the people who enact the ritual."[9] It is important to recognize that what is going on in liturgy is not only for the church but for the world. If the liturgy and especially the Eucharist makes the church, then the church exists in liturgy to point up and to demonstrate the final destiny of all creation.

Now come listening and speaking. Just as there is a primacy at the ordinary human level given to listening in the formation of the person, so too there is a primacy of listening in the Body of Christ, in the gathered assembly of the church. This is the Liturgy of the Word, the readings from holy scripture accompanied by the homily. This is active listening. As in any dialogue or conversation, no listening is ever purely passive, and so as we listen in the Liturgy of the Word, we are active in probing the meaning of what we hear. Robert Barron writes, "Christians discover who God is, what constitutes the sacred world, who they are and ought to be, precisely by listening to the oddly textured narratives of the Bible. They learn to be holy by attending to the cast of characters—saints, rogues, prophets, sinners—on display in the biblical stories, and especially by watching the great Character who acts, sometimes directly, sometimes indirectly, in every story."[10] The meaning of the scriptures does not fall easily into our laps, as it were. We have to work at it, develop our scriptural curiosity, probe the meaning not only of the immediate meetings themselves but also contextually in the whole of the holy scriptures. *That* is active listening. We respond with speech. Ordinary human language is regulated by grammar and syntax. Ecclesial language, that is, language in the church's liturgy, is also regulated by its own ecclesial grammar and syntax. Just as there is no such thing as a private language, so the ecclesial language as a public language must also have a degree of regulation. So, we respond to the Liturgy of the Word in words of prayer and psalmody and in hymns. These provide our ecclesial and liturgical grammar in order that our response may be both intelligible and harmonious. Eating and drinking are next. Eating and drinking are so fundamental that they find a ritual location in many world religions. Many faiths have developed forms of food and drink as ways of sustaining and developing relationship with God. In that sense, Christianity is not especially novel. What is novel is that we are fed with the divine reality. Christians are fed at the Table of the Word and the Table of the Eucharist, "at the twinned tables in the refectory of the Incarnate Logos, one for his word, the other for his flesh."[11] In and through God's grace we become what we eat. And the eating and drinking are essential. Robert Barron writes, "We are meant not simply to admire the Lamb of God, but to consume him, making him bone of our bone and flesh of our flesh."[12]

Finally comes the dismissal. Just as dismissal marks the key moments in the life cycle of every person, dismissal marks the ritual moments in the life cycle of the church. The final words of the Eucharist, proclaimed by the deacon or the priest, are "The Mass is ended. Go in peace." We are sent forth, we are dismissed to be in the world what we have further expressed and become in the assembly, the Body of Christ. We are dismissed to be that Body in our own circumstances, in our own place. That is an enormous challenge, a challenge that is well expressed by Louis Bouyer: "Perhaps the greatest, and certainly the most difficult problem for liturgical piety is the one which awaits us when we go out of the church after the liturgical celebration is finished….The liturgical celebration itself implies a correlative importance in what we do, after the liturgical celebration, in daily living."[13] The quality of daily living as the Body of Christ authenticates and verifies the quality of the ritual and liturgical participation of the Body of Christ.

Conclusion

It might be asked, "Why do we need the Eucharist to rehearse for us what it means to be human?" My response is to suggest that for very many people life is hard, complex, and often immensely challenging. By having every week or even more often in the Eucharist the opportunity to reflect seriously on what it really means to be a human being might help keep us focused, on target, less anxious. Perhaps…

As well as that, thinking along these lines leads us to a much greater appreciation of this radical and mysterious ritual. So, by way of conclusion to this reflection on the Eucharist as life, I want to call upon the witness of Fr. Timothy Radcliffe, OP, former master-general of the Dominicans. These are his very moving words:

> As the years have gone by, I have also learned to love the celebration of the Eucharist. It's the moment—which has become central to my life and to my theology—when you enact the drama that is at the heart of God's relationship with humanity: God places himself in our hands as an absolute gift. The priest's role is not taking Jesus' place so as to become the focus of attention. In a way, the priest ought to disappear; in any case, he should not stand out and point to himself. He is there to help the reenactment of the drama when Jesus surrenders himself entirely into our hands. It's a moment of generosity, of free gift, of pure vulnerability, and it never ceases to amaze me.[14]

Many people, when they stand back from life and reflect on it, find it simply amazing in so many different ways. When you think about it, it is amazing that we exist! The amazement is no less real when it comes to the Eucharist. There we realize that God has become flesh in Jesus, that Jesus has become sacramentally present to us in the eucharistic gifts, in order that we may be divinized. There we realize also that the Eucharist rehearses for us in ritual mode all the constituent elements of what it means to be human. The Eucharist is life.

The Eucharist as Theodicy: Through the Eucharistic Lens of Margaret Spufford

Christian thought about suffering cannot be reduced to explaining it away, in however philosophically sophisticated a way. It must rather embrace the fact that suffering lies at the heart of its formative story.
Frances M. Young[1]

Introduction

Our opening words come from the Methodist theologian Frances M. Young. She is known not only for her many distinguished contributions to patristic theological scholarship but also for her personal struggle with theodicy. One of her sons, Arthur, has suffered most severe developmental difficulties throughout his life, and this has led her to explore in a very personal fashion the meaning of pain and suffering for a Christian, what she has called a "narrative theology of suffering."[2] Such a narrative theodicy stands head and shoulders, it seems to me, over a conceptual theodicy. Many theologians today—for example, John Thiel, Terrence Tilley, Kenneth Surin—view such abstract conceptual attempts at theodicy with increasing skepticism.[3] I do not see how such conceptual attempts may be avoided if theology is to be understood along Anselmian lines as "faith seeking understanding," but perhaps they may be thought of as secondary rather than primary responses to the realities of pain and suffering. Abstract conceptual theodicies can represent, as Paul Crowley puts it, "a calculus about suffering that fails to take into consideration the actual suffering of human beings. As such, theodicies devalue practical issues surrounding evil: they silence the cries of victims and marginalize their suffering; tend to valorize some forms of evil and minimize others; and ultimately promote complicity in injustice because systemic evils such as racism and sexism are rendered invisible."[4] It would be difficult to disagree. Nonetheless, if such theodical attempts were thought of as secondary, perhaps we might move forward with a humble confidence, not explaining away suffering, but rather recognizing it at the very heart of the Christian story.

Such humble confidence may be found in the reflection of historian Margaret Spufford. Historians pay careful attention to detail. As they seek to reach judgments about the past, they scrutinize the accumulated detailed data about the event, the circumstances, the period with which they are dealing from a variety of perspectives, and they reach toward mature and balanced conclusions that do justice to the evidence. Margaret Spufford is a well-known English historian who specializes in the seventeenth century. She wrote a book entitled *Celebration* after the death of her daughter, Bridget, in 1989.[5] If this book is to be thought of as a theodicy, it certainly does not fall under the strictures of Paul Crowley. *Celebration* is not an architectonic account of suffering, an abstract conceptual theodicy. While Frances Young may present us with a narrative account of suffering, Margaret Spufford does more. She presents us with a eucharistic account. In this reflection I scroll through her *Celebration* to find a segue into thinking about the Eucharist as theodicy.

Scrolling through *Celebration*

The book ends with this paragraph:

Two days after I returned home after writing this book, our daughter [Bridget] became ill with what was eventually diagnosed as a neurological failure....Her decline was in no sense amusing. However, she was given the gift of clarity and serenity in the last month of her life and was precisely aware of what was happening and to Whom she was going. It was a month which all four of us [Margaret, her husband, her son, and her daughter, Bridget] were mainly able to spend in her bedroom at home, reading aloud, listening to music, and surrounded by flowers. She died in all our arms, very soon after her twenty-second birthday on the Sunday after Ascension Day, 1989.[6]

The paragraph is revealing. It describes the difficult death of Bridget: "Her decline was in no sense amusing." It describes also, may I say, the beauty of Bridget's death within the bosom of her family, with "the gift of clarity and serenity...in her bedroom at home, reading aloud, listening to music, and surrounded with flowers." Notice also that Bridget was aware of "to Whom she was going." It was an awareness not only of what was happening to her in the illness, but also of the God who was there and who was Bridget's final end. Notice too how the date of Bridget's death is given: "the Sunday after Ascension Day, 1989." The liturgical reference clues us into the deeply Christian context of this dying and death.

Throughout the book Margaret Spufford offers her sensitive Christian commentary on the experience of living for so long, faithfully and lovingly, with her daughter's illnesses. Describing pain and suffering, the sign of the cross in human life, is in a sense so much easier than describing joy and glory, the sign of the resurrection. "Even painters cannot, with the possible exception of Fra Angelico, paint Heaven. Hell, or the fear of it, comes more easily off the brush. Three and a half of the four walls of fourteenth century frescoes by the significantly titled 'Master of the Triumph of Death' in Pisa, are given over to Death, Judgment and Hell: only half a wall attempts Paradise, and that is strangely inept."[7] The ineptitude of painting Paradise surely springs from its distance-in-hope from the enormity of human suffering. We see the joys of Paradise so very,

very darkly, in a mirror. We see the at times overwhelming reality of suffering, pain, dying, and death "face to face." There is no evasion of the reality in Margaret Spufford.

As a result of twenty-two years of suffering with, in, and through Bridget's pain and suffering, she writes:

> God does not defend his people from worldly evil, and he seems powerless or unwilling to protect them. The trust one has to develop in him lies far deeper, in the knowledge that he will be present in the deepest waters, and the most acute pain, and in some apprehension of his will to transform these things. No cheap belief in him as "insurance" will serve....To put oneself trustingly into the hands of God, when one knows his power to break, or allow one to be broken, is difficult.[8]

These are very powerful but immensely difficult words, as the last sentence makes starkly clear. The theologically minded will find the first sentence especially challenging: "God does not defend his people from worldly evil, and he seems powerless or unwilling to protect them." Theologians may be tempted to rush too quickly to God's defense, to develop subtle, metaphysical arguments demonstrating the simultaneous coexistence of the good and loving and almighty God with the facts of suffering and pain. This is the enterprise of *theodicy*, the justification of the good and loving God in the face of so much suffering, "conceptual theodicy."[9] Without abandoning human intelligence, the "unrestricted desire to understand," as Canadian Jesuit theologian Bernard Lonergan puts it, one must admit the need of constructing theodicies. Theodicy as a conceptual construct, however, remains at a very great distance from the immediacy of suffering. Spufford seems to me entirely right to say that a deep trust in God is invited, not an intellectually arrived-at trust on its own, but a trust that reaches in an almost tactile way into the reality of God, "put[ting] oneself trustingly into the hands of God."

This leads Margaret Spufford to conclude:

> I cannot reconcile the images of tiny, deformed children with old men's eyes, in great pain (children who shrank from human contact because so often it represented more pain, the stab of a therapeutic needle which they could not recognize as therapeutic), with what I am bound to believe of a loving, omnipotent Father. I will not assent to all this pain as anything but a manifest evil. One of the commonest Christian heresies is surely to glorify suffering as somehow "good."…I have searched for a theological answer. I do not believe there is one. Would, or can, any theologian produce any answer other than that we are here in the presence of a mystery, insoluble in human terms?[10]

There we have *one* basis of this putting oneself trustingly into the hands of God, the recognition of the presence of sheer mystery, in the strictest sense of the word.

This is no capitulation to absurdity on her part. She returns to the traditional creedal epithet of God as almighty, as all powerful. "The definition of 'Almighty' means that there is no evil out of which good cannot be brought. This I have found, extremely painfully, to be true."[11] The classical Christian understanding of God as "Almighty" does not remain at a logically abstract level, that is to say, if God is "Creator" and not therefore "creature," God must be Almighty since creatures are anything but that. The logic of that is conceptually obvious up to a point. Rather, Spufford brings "Almighty" within the reach of the deep, existential trust of putting oneself into the hands of God: there *is* no evil out of which God cannot bring good. It is a deep, existential conclusion, a conclusion that she has found "extremely painful, to be true." That is the extremely painful truth of the Paschal Mystery that is our Lord Jesus Christ. There can be no persuasive glossing of the fact that the crucified Jesus experienced profoundly the evils of pain and suffering on the cross. He died. Death did not have the final word. Resurrection followed. "The definition of 'Almighty' means that there is no evil out of which good cannot be brought." The good, the final good of resurrection is brought by God out of the evil, the penultimate evil of death. Or, as Spufford once put it in a sermon preached on Passion Sunday at St. Edward's Church, Cambridge, "Good Friday is not the end of Holy Week."[12] That brings us to Spufford's eucharistic reflections, the *second* basis of putting oneself trustingly in the hands of God.

The Eucharist in *Celebration*

> At first sight a book which is about physical or mental pain may seem very oddly titled *Celebration*. But it is written by a woman to whom, over the years, participation in the Eucharist has become the most important part of living, and being in silence before the reserved sacrament the most important part of prayer. Gradually, and with immense diffidence, I have come to see that my own participation in this offering of the Eucharist must involve the presentation of my own experience, for hallowing, along with "the best bread that can conveniently be gotten," in the hope that it, too, can be redeemed and transformed.[13]

This is a profound eucharistic perspective. Three key issues emerge. First, participation in the Eucharist is, for Spufford, "the most important part of living." From what has already been described there is simply no evasion in this utterance. Her living has been marked by the sign of the cross, as has Bridget's. Her ongoing participation in the Eucharist, we may say, has conjoined the deepest pain and suffering, the cross, with the "darkly seen" joy of resurrection. She has come to see this in her own words "gradually, and with immense diffidence." It is no easy insight. It is insight that comes from seeing darkly, but from the continual and regular seeing darkly that is the Eucharist.

Second, and following from her participation in the Eucharist, the most important part of prayer is for her "in silence before the reserved sacrament." Contemplative moments, at times harshly contemplative moments in eucharistic adoration prolong her eucharistic participation. Spufford reiterates a wisdom long held in the Western Christian tradition. The Benedictine theologian Jeremy Driscoll exemplifies what Spufford is alluding to here: "a meditative contemplation of what is too difficult to grasp and digest all at once during Mass. In prayer before the Blessed Sacrament, I am continuing in quiet reflection my communion with Christ from Mass, and I am preparing for the next communion...."[14] The reserved Eucharist is the Mass held in meditation. It takes time to appropriate the entire meaning, and as noted, at times the harshly appropriated meaning of the eucharistic event. In similar vein the French Jesuit theologian Jean-Marie Hennaux writes, "I can only hope to participate in [the Love of Christ] by also adoring it outside myself, thus plainly recognizing that he is, he alone, the *source* of love, the source that I am not. If I would adore him only in his immanence in me [at the moment of my eucharistic communion], I would perhaps risk forgetting his transcendence. My practice of eucharistic communion therefore leads me, in order that I might respect its total mystery, to the adoration of the host outside of me."[15] Spufford does not use Hennaux's language, but she knows his meaning.

Third, she affirms that her own experience of pain and suffering, conjoined to that of Jesus Christ in the eucharistic offering, hopes for and awaits redemption and transformation. God has brought the good of resurrection out of the death of Jesus. "Good Friday is not the end of Holy Week." God will bring good out of this experience of Margaret Spufford's Good Friday of pain and suffering. This is similar to the point of view of the great Karl Rahner, SJ, who once wrote, "It seems to me that even today and in the future we must not forget what our Christian forebears practiced. The sanctuary lamp of our Catholic churches continues to invite us to a silent lingering before the mystery of our redemption."[16] This is exactly what Spufford is doing, but as an Anglican Catholic, not a Roman Catholic. She continues in what might be called "an anonymously Rahnerian" vein: "There is a completeness about attentive silence in the presence of God that leaves nothing else for me to desire. I am so ashamed that so often idleness or busyness and a lack of sense of priorities squeeze out the time in which I could at least put myself in the way of achieving this stillness….There is a completeness about adoration: the soul is stilled in the presence of God, there is nothing left to desire."[17]

The Eucharist as Performative Theodicy

Let me cite one final passage from Margaret Spufford's *Celebration* on the Eucharist:

> The center of this pain, and also of this silence and light, lies in the Eucharist. Sometimes we are ill served by familiarity. Even the language of the original events that we re-enact, Eucharist by Eucharist, has become so familiar to us that it has lost some of its force, partly through constant repetition. From the phraseology of picking up our cross, and following our Lord, we have to strip all the clothing of habit, take it back to its original meaning, and think of his torture and of his death on a gibbet. Sometimes I cannot understand our external placidity, as we stand there, faced now, afresh, with the agony of this death, and the flies on these wounds. The reenactment is a burning-glass, focusing pain, drawing together all those screams I have heard, all those broken branches and bruised flowers, all those fossils in the Grand Canyon, all the fears I have for my own future of cumulative fracture. There is nothing, ultimately, nothing, that I can do of myself to transform all this pain. There have been times I wanted to scream…and I have not been able to bear to go [to Holy Communion] at all. I do remember how once my own pain was transformed for me by pure gift, by the presence of the Crucified….But it is because the celebration of the Eucharist and Christ's offering of him-

self in it seems to comprehend all the realities of acute pain and death that I have not handed in my ticket.[18]

Once again in this passage we see no evasion of the horror and the enormity of pain and suffering. The pain and suffering of the entire cosmos, her own personal narrative of pain and suffering, the suffering of the Lord Jesus on the cross, re-presented in the Eucharist. There is a reference to Dostoyevsky in his book *The Brothers Karamazov*. There Ivan Karamazov speaks about handing in his ticket to God if the suffering of the innocent is to be justified somehow through some philosophically abstract theodicy. It is clear that Spufford identifies with Ivan in refusing such theodicy. It is no less clear that she finds her hope in "the celebration of the Eucharist and Christ's offering himself in it." There is further similarity to the thought of Karl Rahner in this passage: "[The Eucharist] is a sacrament which is meant to ensure that we live more and more 'in Him' and become ever more like Him. Must not the holy Eucharist then draw us ever more deeply also into the mystery of the cross of Christ?...The Eucharist, moreover, renews the memory of the sufferings of Christ even by letting Christ's sufferings flow over to us together with grace."[19]

Perhaps we might call this "performative theodicy." Christians do not have an entirely persuasive intellectual response to the challenges of evil, pain, and suffering. This is what I mean by an abstract conceptual theodicy. In the Eucharist, and missioned at the end of the Eucharist—"Go in peace..."—they perform a response. Incorporated into and conjoined with the presence of the Crucified in the Eucharist, they live out a theodicy. It is never evasive, never looking for some cheap solution. It is crucifyingly costly. While this performative theodicy is primary, the enterprise of thinking these things through intellectually remains, but it is secondary. The Eucharist is the primary Christian theodicy.

Benediction: Its History and Theology

I put before you the one great thing to love on earth: the Blessed Sacrament....There you will find romance, glory, fidelity, and the true way of all your loves on earth, and much more besides.

J. R. R. Tolkien[1]

It seems to me that even today and in the future we must not forget what our Christian forebears practiced. The sanctuary lamp of our Catholic churches continues to invite us to a silent lingering before the mystery of our redemption.

Karl Rahner, SJ[2]

History of Benediction

Benediction is a devotion consisting in the exposition of the Sacred Host on the altar and, after the singing of appropriate hymns, a blessing with the Sacred Host. As a devotional practice, Benediction developed at the time when the elevation of the consecrated gifts was introduced into the Mass and the celebration of the feast of Corpus Christi into the Christian year.[3]

Sometime between 1205 and 1208 a synod was held at Paris by the bishop Odo of Sully to deal with certain questions of eucharistic theology and liturgical practice. One of the synod's decisions was that the host was to be elevated after the consecration so that it might be seen by the people; it also settled the disputed question about the precise moment of consecration.[4] Was the host consecrated after the words *Hoc est enim corpus meum* were pronounced or only after the dominical words over the chalice? The synod, undoubtedly after consultation with the Parisian masters of theology, settled on the former, and so mandated the elevation of the host after the words over the bread. In all probability, this showing of the host during Mass was strengthened and confirmed by its showing at the various stations of the Corpus Christi procession. The elevation and showing of the host seems to have been a response to the growing desire of the faithful to gaze upon the host.

After the reaffirmation of Catholic belief in the real presence of Christ against the reformers in the Council of Trent (1545–63), "churches tended to be built whose interior lines focused the eye upon the tabernacle (placed directly upon the altar), and upon the throne provided at the heart of the reredos for the monstrance."[5] And so, Benediction passed into regular Catholic life from the Council of Trent to Vatican II (1962–65), but not without a certain reserve and caution.

Writing in the *New Catholic Encyclopedia* in 1967, the Benedictine scholar Maur Burbach makes the following caution about Benediction: "The emphasis upon Benediction, as we know the devotion today, is not without certain dangers. The church has always been hesitant to give free rein to it, as is evident from the restrictions, gradually lessened, of its use."[6] Burbach's statement sounds a little strange until we recognize the historical facts that lie behind it.

Historically, in the period after the Council of Trent, the church entertained a certain reserve about eucharistic exposition, described by Nathan Mitchell as follows: "The authoritative regulation of such practices generally took the form of restriction and limitation, rather than positive encouragement."[7] The Sacred Congregation for Rites was cautious because of a fear of abuse. This cautious approach was to figure for a long time. For example, it is reported that at the Plenary Council held at Fort Augustus in

1886, Scottish parish priests were forbidden to give eucharistic Benediction without the explicit permission of the local bishop.[8] Despite this caution, however, "the period after Trent was marked by a multiplication of devotional customs."[9]

What abuses did the Sacred Congregation for Rites and episcopal conferences fear? Dom Burbach goes on to point out some of the excesses that needed to be guarded against in the celebration of this devotion: the substitution of Benediction for Mass, or its celebration with more solemnity than Mass itself, or allowing it to replace Vespers. One might also add the possible reaction to Jansenism, which had a particular interest in eucharistic adoration.[10] In fact, the first Roman document to declare Benediction to be a true liturgical action came as late as 1958 with the *Instruction on Sacred Music and Liturgy*.

The introduction of the possibility of evening Masses in the 1960s, among other things, probably led to the quasi-demise of Benediction, as Benediction had most often been an evening act of eucharistic worship and adoration. Without its being intentional, the easy accessibility to the Mass, morning and evening, led to its being made to bear almost the complete burden of Catholic devotion, and deliberately or indeliberately to the virtual demise in some places of Benediction. This may also have been advanced by the increased questioning of the value of contemplation in some Catholic circles in the late 1960s.

A revised Rite of Eucharistic Exposition and Benediction was included in the Roman document *Holy Communion and Worship of the Eucharist outside Mass* (1973). It is very clear, and indeed traditional, about the purpose of eucharistic reservation: "The primary and original reason for Reservation of the Eucharist outside Mass is the administration of viaticum. The secondary reasons are the giving of Communion and the adoration of our Lord Jesus Christ who is present in the sacrament."[11] The document is equally emphatic that eucharistic devotions should be understood to flow from the liturgy and to lead to the liturgy: "Devotions should be in harmony with the sacred liturgy in some sense, take their origin from the liturgy, and lead people back to the liturgy."[12] Not only is there no conflict with the official liturgy of the church, but also, such devotions find their meaning in and from the liturgy. To illustrate something of this, let me now turn to an Anglican theologian, John Macquarrie, whose appreciation of Benediction is second to none.

The Experience of John Macquarrie

John Macquarrie (1919–2007), Emeritus Lady Margaret Professor of Divinity in the University of Oxford and the premier Anglican systematic theologian of the twentieth century, wrote a fine essay on Benediction that is as worth reading today as it was when first published almost forty-five years ago in a journal and then again in 1972.[13] The essay is valuable not only for what it has to say about the theology of Benediction, but also because it is rooted in Macquarrie's own experience while he was still a Presbyterian, a minister of the Church of Scotland. While waiting in a transit area in London to be posted overseas to Egypt just after World War II, Macquarrie found himself wandering into the Anglican Church of St. Andrews, Willesden Green. The bell was ringing for Evensong and Benediction. Let us read his experience of the latter in his own words: "No doubt I was in an impressionable mood that night but this service meant a great deal to me. Evensong had already meant much, but now, as it were, an additional dimension, was also opened up. I did not know what lay ahead of me or when I might come back to these shores again, but I had been assured of our Lord's presence and had received his sacramental blessing."[14]

Macquarrie acknowledges that the Eucharist is the center of all Christian worship. The aim must be "to extend the action and meaning of the Eucharist out from the center to the furthest edges of life, so that the whole of life is conformed to the living Lord who gives himself to us at the altar."[15] He tells us that whenever he had the opportunity to attend Benediction he did so.

Apologia for Benediction

How is this eucharistic devotion to be defended? For Macquarrie, the initial defense lies in the need we humans experience "to have before us some concrete manifestation of the divine reality, toward which we can direct our devotion." He continues, "It is simply a fact of human psychology that the worshipers' awareness of the Lord's presence [is] intensified and brought home in a lively way as they look upon the spotless Host."[16]

There is another aspect to the psychological apologia for Benediction. It is impossible to appropriate in any realistic fashion the meaning of the Eucharist during the short time of its celebration. If the personal appropriation of the "mysterial movement" of the Eucharist is to occur, and it is surely desirable that it does, there is a need for meditative eucharistic prayer such as Benediction.[17]

The defense of the practice, however, does not remain at the psychological level alone. There is also a theology at work. While psychologically we need a visible focus of the Lord's presence, theologically that presence is manifest to us in the Blessed Sacrament. Macquarrie believes—and this reflects the teaching of the Catholic Church—that Benediction is best celebrated after Evensong or Vespers. The reason? Because this sequence brings together the two complementary emphases of word and sacrament. These emphases are inseparable, the one leading necessarily to the other. When they are separated, the Body of Christ is split, as happened in the sixteenth century, with one part of the church seeming to affirm word, the other sacrament. If we have careful regard to the sixth chapter of St. John's Gospel, we will find this work-sacrament nexus of the Eucharist beautifully represented. The first part of John 6 (vv. 1–15) invites us to appreciate the eucharistic multiplication of the loaves. We are told that Jesus "took the loaves, and when he had given thanks, he distributed them to those who were seated" (v. 11). This is the action of the Eucharist: taking, blessing, breaking (implicit here), and distributing. After the brief episode of walking on the water (vv. 16–21), we move into the "Bread of Life Discourse," the word (vv. 22–59). This reaches a conclusion in the magnificent words of Peter: "Lord, to whom can we go? You have the words of eternal life" (v. 68). There can be no Benediction without the celebration of the Eucharist, as in John 6:1–15. The meaning of that action must be unfolded in the word and finally accepted as the words of eternal life. Cardinal Cahal Daly comments on the passage: "It seems idle to analyze the chapter into a mystical section concerned with Christ's word and a sacramental section concerned with Christ's Eucharistic body. The mystical section is Eucharistic and the Eucharistic section is mystical. Word and Eucharist, faith and sacrament, mysticism and liturgy are inseparable for St. John, as they have been for the great Catholic tradition."[18]

If Benediction were prefaced by Vespers, it would afford a special opportunity to recognize and celebrate this word-Eucharist nexus in a way that would enhance the celebration of the Eucharist itself. Indeed, *Holy Communion and Worship of the Eucharist outside Mass* encourages this use of scripture during eucharistic adoration and Benediction: "To encourage a prayerful spirit, there should be readings from Scripture with a homily or brief exhortations to develop a better understanding of the Eucharistic mystery....Part of the Liturgy of the Hours, especially the principal hours, may be celebrated before the Blessed Sacrament when there is a lengthy period of exposition."[19] We may see here on the church's part a desire to bring together for the upbuilding of the church's life, word and sacrament, word and Eucharist, and may we say though perhaps indirectly the varying emphases of the Reformed and Catholic traditions.

The Three Parts of Benediction

Macquarrie suggests that Benediction may helpfully be considered as tripartite: contemplation, sacramental blessing, praise and thanksgiving. First, contemplation. This occurs in the first part of the service when the sacrament is exposed in the mon-

92

strance and the traditional eucharistic hymns—*O Salutaris Hostia* and *Tantum Ergo*—are sung. It is a moment of contemplation of Christ's saving presence. Macquarrie considers that we human beings are much too busy, and indeed, even our worship may be at times too busy: "While the modern liturgical movement has rightly tried to wean people away from the notion that they are spectators or auditors at worship, it has, I believe, stressed too much what *we* do, and too little what *comes to us from God*. It is good for us just to let God soak into us, so to speak...."[20]

Second, sacramental blessing. This is the blessing of the people with the monstrance. When the sign of the cross is made with the monstrance over the people following the moment of contemplation, this blessing means that "God is always ahead of us, and our worship is response."[21] The priority is always with grace. God takes the initiative and comes to us before we turn to him.

Third, praise and thanksgiving. This is the response of prayer known as the "Divine Praises." Here is the text of the prayer:

> Blessed be God.
> Blessed be his holy name.
> Blessed be Jesus Christ, true God and true man.
> Blessed be the name of Jesus.
> Blessed be his most Sacred Heart.
> Blessed be his most Precious Blood.
> Blessed be Jesus in the most holy Sacrament of the altar.
> Blessed be the Holy Spirit, the Paraclete.
> Blessed be the great Mother of God, Mary most holy.
> Blessed be her holy and Immaculate Conception.
> Blessed be her glorious Assumption.
> Blessed be the name of Mary, virgin and mother.
> Blessed be St. Joseph, her most chaste spouse.
> Blessed be God in his angels and in his saints.

The prayer is a particular condensation of the creed. It begins with God the Father: "Blessed be God. Blessed be his holy name." It moves on to Christ—"Blessed be Jesus Christ, true God and true man"—and to the other christological statements. The Holy Spirit is then acknowledged, followed by the church in the persons of Mary and Joseph. The prayer ends with an inclusion, "Blessed be God," but this time with "his angels and his saints." More theologically, we might say that the prayer is trinitarian, christological, pneumatological, ecclesiological, and eschatological. Let us turn to some of these elements in a little more detail.

God the Father is blessed and then "his holy name." Shortly afterward, "the name of Jesus" is also blessed. *Name* is an important term in the Divine Praises. What does it mean? Name is identity. When we are introduced to someone by name, we are invited to share something of their identity by entering into relationship with them. The name of the Father is blessed, is holy and gracious, reaching out to us to enrich us, and equally the name of the Son is blessed. The prayer, in naming Father and Son as blessed, is first acknowledging the utter priority of God as Father in our regard and inviting the deepening and strengthening of our relationship with the Father in the Son. I put it this way because, quite simply, there is no Son without us, the church. We are sons and daughters in the Son, so that the Divine Praises, in naming that relationship, also invite and enable its strengthening and deepening.

The christological parts of the prayer focus first of all on the affirmation of the Council of Chalcedon (451) that Jesus is *homoousios*/one in being with the Father, and one in being with us, sin alone excepted. He is "true God and true man." Mention is next made of his great love for us, his Sacred Heart, and of the sacrificial dimensions of that love, his most Precious Blood. The word *heart* appears in the Old Testament about one thousand times, and in the New Testament about one hundred and fifty times.[22] Summarizing the complex biblical usage of the word *heart*, Joachim Becker writes, "The heart is the locus of everything that is innermost, genuine, precious and essential in men, all that is the opposite of empty superficiality."[23] Perhaps we could say that the heart is the core of the person reaching out to others in all their fullness, in all their depth. The scriptures also say about thirty times that God has a heart. The paucity of references in contrast to the other statistics may reflect traditional biblical reluctance to say much about God's innermost reality, but perhaps we may say that talk of God's heart is talk of God reaching out in love and concern to others. In connection with the next prayer, "Blessed be his most Precious Blood," Jesus is the heart that loved others, and loved them *eis telos*/to the end, to the point where self-donation has nothing left. The shedding of his Precious Blood was the *telos*, the end beyond which there is nowhere to go.

Superficially, it may seem that the Holy Spirit gets short shrift in the Divine Praises, with but one *makarism*/blessing given over to him, but this is untrue. Behind the verbally laconic references to the Holy Spirit in our Roman Catholic tradition lies the foundational conviction of St. Paul: "No one can say 'Jesus is Lord,' except by the Holy Spirit" (1 Cor 12:3). All our spiritual and theological conferences are Spirit breathed, *Theopneustos*, because the Spirit is the soul of the church's body, making and giving life and enabling us to pray what we pray. When the church praises, or any of her members praise, the Spirit is producing the prayer and, so, is always present.

Just as the first reference to the Lord retrieves the definition of Chalcedon, "true God and true man," so the first reference to our Blessed Lady retrieves the Council of Ephesus's (431) famous affirmation that she is *Theotokos*/God bearer and, therefore, most holy. Hence her Immaculate Conception, utterly graced by way of anticipation of the redemption from the beginning, and her glorious Assumption her finalization in heavenly beatitude. Her spouse, St. Joseph, has a mention, thereby reaffirming Mary's humanity and the biblical record that Joseph was *dikaois*/just, one of the saints. Finally, the entire heavenly company is acknowledged in the final prayer, "Blessed be God in his angels and in his saints."

Conclusion

John Macquarrie speaks of "the missionary pull of Benediction."[24] A most interesting phrase! What does he mean by this?

For Macquarrie, the solemnity and beauty of Benediction has the power to draw people—even people who may not be baptized—to a sense of God's holy presence. What, however, about Catholics? In an age when eucharistic devotions are not only challenged but at times marginalized, how would one assess the value of Benediction in the Christian life? Are there criteria for such assessment? I think there are three basic and fundamental criteria. First, does Benediction increase my love for the celebration of the Eucharist, for more careful preparation for the celebration? Do I find myself wanting to receive holy communion more frequently and more devoutly? Second, does Benediction form me closer in relationship and personal encounter with the Lord? Is my spiritual experience as the result of Benediction about being drawn before the Father, in the Son, through the Holy Spirit? Third, do I find myself impelled to works of charity, to a sense of eucharistic mission as a consequence of being in prayer before the Lord's sacramental presence in Benediction? If the answers to these questions are in the affirmative, then Benediction is all that it ought to be in my life.

10

Reconciliation: Through the Lenses of Two Novelists

People are much sadder than they seem.

St. John Vianney, Curé d'Ars

The wisdom of the religions is clear: by hurting others we wound our own heart more terribly than by anything others can inflict on us. This is almost unimaginable, to think that being nasty to someone is worse for us than suffering them being nasty to us. It is not true that the worst thing that can happen to us is being wronged, wounded or even killed: the worst thing is to do wrong. The double tragedy is that our wounds, which can be so terrible, are often an almost irresistible temptation to inflict wounds on others.

David F. Ford[1]

Each of us lives with a radical sense of not being fulfilled and satisfied because of things we have said and done and left unsaid and undone, and not just because we have unfulfilled aspirations in life. This is the dysfunction of sin, what the great Cardinal Henri de Lubac, SJ, called "this mysterious limp" from which we all suffer. Everyone knows about this limp. Robert Barron describes the limp most egregiously at work nationally and personally: "Never forgetting, never forgiving, never recovering from past offences, people around the globe allow their lust for vengeance to well up unchecked. And the same phenomenon can be seen in families and communities where grudges are borne for decades, even when the originating offence is long forgotten."[2] All Catholics need to

97

avail themselves of the sacrament of penance and reconciliation. We know in our bones our need of it.

Reconciliation is a deeply Christian word, with a long history. "Reconciliation is a complex biblical term which includes God's invitation and our response to ongoing conversion within a community of faith."[3] As we respond to the divine invitation, we become increasingly aware of our inadequacies, our failures and flaws, our sins. The most obvious meaning of reconciliation for a Catholic is probably the sacrament of penance and reconciliation. The regular experience of this sacrament is so important that I cannot underscore it adequately. It ought to be a key component of our spiritual lives, our lives in Christ. At the same time, it is important to have a bigger picture of reconciliation in which our own personal experience of the sacrament may find its place, indeed may become the animator of our practice of reconciliation. One author writes, "Reconciliation is too grand to be limited to a sacrament....Our tradition supports the view that reconciliation is really the core metaphor or way to describe what Christians believe about the unique activity of Jesus the Christ himself."[4]

"It is ultimately in our own best interests that we become forgiving, repentant, reconciling, and reconciled people, because without forgiveness, without reconciliation, we have no future."[5] These words of Archbishop Desmond Tutu run like a refrain throughout his book *No Future without Forgiveness*, in which he tells the story and context of South Africa's Truth and Reconciliation Commission. In South Africa, after apartheid had been dismantled and Nelson Mandela led the country into a new democratic shape, the remembered atrocities of the former era could easily have brought about an almost completely destructive situation. That did not occur.

> What happened in South Africa was unique, a "third way" between the extremes of vengeance and national amnesia, consisting of an amnesty granted to all those, whether freedom fighters or instruments of the apartheid regime,

who confessed their gross human rights violations. It should be noted that the requirement for amnesty was not that they show remorse but that they confess, as it was reasoned that it would be impossible to look into the hearts of those testifying and determine the presence or absence of remorse.[6]

What a wise decision, since, despite our suspicions and detailed observations, no one really knows the interiority of another. Though we cannot see remorse necessarily, we can hear confession of sin and wrongdoing.

How are we to think of reconciliation and what it presupposes, estrangement? I think that very basically we relate to and treat one another either as gift or as threat:

We can discover all life and existence, especially our fellow human beings, as precious gift. We can realize, however much it costs us to do so, that the discovery of all life and existence as precious gift is equally accessible to all. We can then discover how cherished and consequently how precious are all our fellow humans. We can accept all and enrich others as we have been enriched. And then life is positive, full, enhanced with hope of limitless possibilities. Sometimes, to some extent, all this is true of ourselves and our lives.

But we can also try to tear life and existence free from the hands of the giver, try to appropriate it, to draw it entirely under our own dominion....We will then divide ourselves against ourselves....The barriers will go up, at once our defenses and our prisons; suspicion and hostility will breed fear and further insecurity. And then life will be diminished in quality, fragile in our consciousness of it, threatened. Only too often, to a great extent, all this is true of ourselves and our lives.

This is where we feel unreconciled to our fellows and our world...suffering from some increasing sickness in our spirits—in need of reconciliation, ransom, acquittal, healing.[7]

These are the words of theologian James P. Mackey, and they are good. What Mackey is saying is admirably clear. Under God's grace we are enabled habitually to recognize everyone as gift, and then we flourish—some of the time; or we can recognize habitually the other as threat, and both we and the other are diminished—too much of the time. Gift and threat, reconciliation and estrangement. None of us, it seems to me, gets this right. We see the other person only from our own angle of vision, only from our own perspective, and an angle of vision and perspective that is self-evidently limited and only too obviously flawed.

Perhaps we can get a better sense of the theology of reconciliation and its fruits if we turn to the world of imagination, the world of fiction. In particular, I have in mind the recent novel of the Irish writer Nuala O'Faolain, *My Dream of You,*[8] and the novel of the American writer Anne Tyler, *Saint Maybe.*[9] Having read O'Faolain's 528-page novel, I suspect that it is quite autobiographical, in part revealing something of her own story. Be that as it may, the novel is a narrative of threat becoming gift, of estrangement giving way to reconciliation. The main character is Kathleen De Burca, an Irish woman who is now fifty, unmarried, and who has just quit her job as a travel journalist working for a prestigious travel magazine. Although born and brought up in Ireland, Kathleen has lived in London for twenty-eight years. During that time she has never gone back, or we might say that she has never gone home, as an exile might put it. She hasn't gone home because she is estranged from her family, her country, her religious faith, and, throughout, from herself. She is estranged from the De Burca family, a dysfunctional family if ever there was one. The father spends almost no time with his children. He is a civil servant, working in Dublin where he would spend the week, coming back at the weekend—I don't say coming home—because he is so remote from the real tortured texture of the De Burca family lives. His wife, Kathleen's mother, is a very depressed woman who seems unable to care for herself or her children. She spends most of the day in bed, doesn't clean, doesn't cook. She lacks self-esteem, and while her husband and she may have been in love at one time, she seems bound now in a union of loveless sex and complete dependence on her husband. The mother dies of uterine cancer, and Kathleen does not return for the funeral. She blames her father for not caring for her mother. Her younger brother dies, and she refuses to go back. Her father also dies, but she does not go home. She pretty much gives up the practice of her Catholic faith, not so much denying God or the church as just drifting away from practice. Kathleen sums up her life in these words: "I have never taken an unhurried look at the people by whom I was formed, wanting nothing but to see clearly....My family has been the same size since I ran out of Ireland. Mother? Victim. Nora and me and Danny and poor little Sean? Neglected victims of her victimhood. Villain? Father. Old-style Irish Catholic patriarch; unkind to wife, unloving to children, harsh to young Kathleen when she tried to talk to him."[10]

Kathleen's own life has been quite empty. Quite successful in terms of her career, she has had a number of lovers, no relationship lasting very long. She wonders why no man finds her companionable to the point of commitment. Being continually on the move, traveling the world for her magazine suits her down to the ground. She loves being on the move, seeing new, different, and exotic places, and meeting new people. Her best friend is one of her colleagues from work, Jimmy. Whatever she has revealed about herself over the course of her life, it has been to this man. He knows her deep estrangement from family, home, and faith, and in his own way, now and again, prompts her reconciliation.

Jimmy dies very suddenly of a heart attack. This death brings about slowly and even indeliberately Kathleen's journey toward reconciliation. She cries out in her pain: "My one and only life slipped past and I never even noticed."[11] She goes back to Ireland, she revisits what family she has left, she pays her respects in the cemetery, she begins to pray, even if in fits and starts. She continues to make mistakes, but she also begins to reach out to help someone who has just been bereaved, whose mother has died, and in reaching out she minimally begins to find something of her parents, her homeland, her faith, herself. As she leaves Ireland again at the end of the book after her visit, Kathleen says, "No one looking at me would guess that I was praying. Let there be a heaven. Let Mammy be in heaven. Let there be something for her because she had such a hard life....Mammy, please if you still exist, please be somewhere where you are loved, and the cold circle of neglect that was around you in life, please let it be burned away."[12] If I had to describe Kathleen De Burca in summary fashion, it would be like this. She has been hurt by life, victimized, she has built walls and barriers to keep others out, she judges those closest to her with an inflexible absoluteness. She is estranged. Slowly, the process of reconciliation heals the hollow of her heart.

Ian Bedloe is the hero of Anne Tyler's *Saint Maybe*, seventeen years old at the beginning of the novel and in his forties by its end. The Bedloe family of Baltimore was a perfect family—an "ideal, apple-pie household" with "golden"-hued children—and with no problems, that is, until the older son, Danny, married a divorcée, Lucy, who has two children. While the Bedloes were getting over that, Lucy gave birth to a child after seven months of marriage, and before marriage she had known Danny only a few weeks. Ian Bedloe is Danny's younger brother. Unreceptive to his new sister-in-law and skeptical that the new child is his brother's, Ian lets Danny know of his suspicions. Danny is a cuckold and a fool. In point of fact, Lucy's infidelity to Danny is "a figment of [Ian's] overheated imagination."[13] But this overheated imagination has terrible consequences. As a result of hearing Ian's suspicions, Danny accelerates a car, crashes, and is killed. Ian realizes that he is responsible for what happened. Lucy is unable to cope after her husband's death, and commits suicide. Now Ian feels that he has two deaths on his hands. In his despair over the situation, he wanders the streets and comes across a church known as "The Church of the Second Chance."

The pastor of this small church is the Reverend Emmett, and it is to this man that Ian confesses his sin. Then he says to the minister, "But, don't you think? Don't you think I'm forgiven?" The minister's response takes Ian by surprise: "Goodness, no," Reverend Emmett said briskly." Ian is surprised because being told he wasn't forgiven seemed to contradict everything he had ever heard or understood about Christianity. The minister goes on to say that God does indeed forgive everything, and then goes on to say, "You can't just say, 'I'm sorry, God.' Why anyone could do that much! You have to offer reparation—concrete practical reparation, according to the rules of our church." The reverend was more than ready to tell him what he must do to make reparation for his sins. He would have "to see to the children." In other words, he tells Ian that it is not good enough to say that you are sorry. No, maintains the pastor, God wants Ian to show he is sorry for what he has done by taking care of the three orphaned children, even if this means his dropping out of college and giving up his own personal plans for life. Here is the passage that follows from the book:

> "Okay. But…see to them in what way exactly?" "Why, raise them, I suppose." "Huh?" Ian said. "But I'm only a freshman!" Reverend Emmett turned to face him, hugging the stack of hymnals against his concave shirt front. "I'm away in Pennsylvania most of the time!" Ian told him. "Then maybe you should drop out." "Drop out?" "Right." "Drop out of college?" "Right." Ian stared at him. "This is some kind of test, isn't it?" he said finally. Reverend Emmett nodded, smiling. Ian sagged with relief. "It's God's test," Reverend Emmett told him.
>
> "So…" "God wants to know how far you'll go to undo the harm you've done." "But he wouldn't really make me follow through with it," Ian said. "How else would he know, then?" "Wait," Ian said, "You're saying God would want me to give up my education. Change all my parents' plans for me and give up my education?"

"Yes, if that's what's required," Reverend Emmett said. "But that's crazy! I'd have to be crazy!" "'Let us not love in word, neither in tongue,'" Reverend Emmett said, "'but in deed and in truth.' 1 John 3:18." "I can't take care of a bunch of kids! Who do you think I am? I'm nineteen years old!" Ian said. "What kind of a cockeyed religion is this?" "It's the religion of atonement and complete forgiveness," Reverend Emmett said. "It's the religion of the Second Chance." Then he set the hymnals on the counter and turned to offer Ian a beatific smile. Ian thought he had never seen anyone so absolutely at peace.[14]

Theologian L. Gregory Jones writes, "Ian comes to recognize that any forgiveness worth having ought to be linked both to repentance and a changed way of life. In so doing, he also recognizes that forgiveness is not simply, and perhaps not even determinatively, about his own guilt. It is also, and more centrally, about the brokenness the sin has created. Ian's 'second chance' involves making amends for that brokenness through concrete reparation."[15] Ian takes full responsibility for raising the children. Eventually, he is able to remember the faces of Danny and Lucy, against whom he has sinned. No longer does he remember only their deaths, but their lives as well, and he also reaches out to forgive himself. "Even with the help of Daphne [the youngest child] and his own life experiences, it takes Ian over twenty years to come to the realization that his actions did not determine Danny and Lucy's death in any final or ultimate way."[16]

There is one other story in this reconciliation anthology. It is the story of God the Father in Luke 15, the parable of the Prodigal Son. The younger son, seeking his father's death in asking for his legacy, goes far astray. Estranged from family and from his native home, from his religious faith, he reaches the pit of human despair. He turns to go back to his father's house. The father, ever watchful and waiting for the tiniest sign of his son's return, runs out to meet him. Pusillanimity and magnanimity meet.

Unworthiness is the understandable filial posture of the son. Pusillanimity is named and owned in the face of magnanimity: "I have sinned against heaven and before you." But the magnanimous and loving father simply wants his son home. That is reconciliation from the father's experiential point of view.

Kathleen De Burca and Ian Bedloe, both fairly ordinary people, both in dire need of reconciliation, both in desperate need of overcoming estrangement. Both Kathleen and Ian have much in common. They are pusillanimous, not magnanimous. Pusillanimity is small-mindedness, thinking that one understands what is going on without qualification, that one has a complete grasp of the situation, as far as others are concerned. One has an inner connection to people's motives and their inner lives, an infallible comprehension of the otherness of the other. There is no room for doubt or ambiguity. Then, both Kathleen and Ian slowly begin to recognize their sin, for that is what pusillanimity is, sin, failure to recognize that God's grace and love are always, but always greater than my puny intellectual capacity to judge. Kathleen and Ian reach toward magnanimity, not in a pelagian way in and through their own abilities, but through God's grace working through others. In God's grace Kathleen comes across a dying librarian, a single lady in the west of Ireland who becomes for her the pedagogue of reconciliation. In God's grace, Ian finds the Church of the Second Chance, whose realistic pastor leads him to recognize the necessity of reparation for true repentance, even at great paschal cost to himself. In both instances reconciliation emerges, slowly but really, for Kathleen and Ian. Reconciliation is neither quick nor cheap. They both know the fruits of reconciliation. They are hope, peace, and a perduring joy. They have become gracefully magnanimous. They have begun to go to their Father's house.

Kathleen De Burca and Ian Bedloe stand as paradigms of reconciliation for us. Their stories are not of their own making, but the product of families, with their graces and faults, the product of the ongoing from original sin of the world. Each one of us is

Kathleen and Ian in our own ways. We are the products of estrangement and lostness, and we are the producers of estrangement and lostness. This seems to me true of every family. The point is, however, that none of us is locked into estrangement and lostness. Reconciliation and being found are gracious gifts to us all. The point is that reconciliation can happen and does work, but somehow I must first search for it and want it.

Reconciled and estranged, gift and threat. We are both. It is certainly more Catholic to recognize the other as gift, and where necessary seek reconciliation with the others from whom we may be estranged. That is what our Father in heaven wants for us, and even though we find that we cannot measure up to the divine expectations, we can daily limp forward. George Herbert again:

> Though I fail, I weep:
> Though I halt in pace,
> > Yet I creep
> To the throne of grace.[17]

In the Gospels, our blessed Lord mentions only one unforgivable sin: blasphemy against the Holy Spirit in Matthew 12:32 (and parallels). What is that unforgivable sin, that blasphemy against the Holy Spirit? There has been a long history of reflection on and speculation about what this means, especially about what makes the sin unforgivable. In the whole context of St. Matthew's Gospel, the unforgivable sin seems to mean the refusal to accept the forgiveness that God always offers. "It is unforgivable because there is no way for us to accept forgiveness if we refuse to acknowledge our own need for forgiveness. Consequently, we quench the Spirit whose work is to enable us to embody forgiveness as we become holy in the light of Christ. Any sin can be forgiven, *if* we are willing to acknowledge the need for forgiveness as well as the need to forgive."[18] It all sounds so passive, but in fact it is very paschal. The fruits of reconciliation, of forgiving others and forgiving ourselves, demand not only that we accept God's hope, peace, and a perduring joy—these are the signs and the fruits of our forgiveness, our reconciliation. We also need effectively to protest against all and any relationships that result in the diminishment or destruction of persons. We must find it intolerable to diminish or destroy others, and we must find it intolerable to observe their diminishment or destruction. Both go hand in hand.

Conclusion

I return to George Herbert, whom we have met several times before in this book, for my conclusion. In the years of his short life he reached, or perhaps better he *was* reached by an overwhelming sense of God as Love, in embrace and reconciliation. This is the poem "Love," the poem that was instrumental in bringing a conversion of heart to the French philosopher Simone Weil, and the poem so wonderfully set to music by the English composer Ralph Vaughan Williams (1872–1958) in his "Five Sacred Songs." This is the very last poem in Herbert's collection; after it he wrote the word *Finis*, "the end." Perhaps he meant the end not only in terms of his time on earth, or of his poetic work, but also the end in the sense that there is no more to be said. The context is eucharistic. God is inviting the soul to the eucharistic banquet, but as the soul enters the presence of Love, he recognizes that he is very unlovely, and yet in his unloveliness God desires him:

> Love bade me welcome: yet my soul drew back,
> > Guilty of dust and sin.
> But quick-ey'd Love, observing me grow slack
> > From my first entrance in,
> Drew nearer to me sweetly questioning,
> > If I lacked any thing.
>
> A guest, I answer'd, worthy to be here:
> > Love said, you shall be he.
> I, the unkind, the ungrateful? Ah, my dear,

I cannot look on thee.
Love took my hand, and smiling did reply,
Who made the eyes but I?
Truth Lord, but I have marr'd them: let my shame
Go where it doth deserve.
And know you not, says Love, who bore the blame?
My dear, then I will serve.
You must sit down, says Love, and taste my meat:
So I did sit and eat.

Sitting and eating at the invitation of the God who is Love, at his eucharistic table, is the climactic experience of reconciliation, is both cause and effect of reconciliation, both means and fruit of reconciliation.

Death and God's Lovely Presence: John Henry Newman and "The Dream of Gerontius"

I suppose every one has a great deal to say about the Providence of God over him. Every one doubtless is so watched over and tended by Him that at the last day, whether he be saved or not, he will confess that nothing could have been done for him more than had been actually done—and every one will feel his own history as special and singular.

Blessed John Henry Newman, in his journal for
June 25, 1869[1]

Very few of the many words penned by John Henry Newman have been set to music. Three compositions, however, have become universally popular in the Christian world: "Lead, Kindly Light," "Firmly I Believe and Truly," and "Praise to the Holiest in the Height." The first stands on its own. The other two are taken from "The Dream of Gerontius." These two poetic pieces, "Lead, Kindly Light" and "The Dream of Gerontius," represent the very best of Newman as a poet. I believe that the very best way into "The Dream of Gerontius" is to listen to the entirety of Sir Edward Elgar's musical setting of "The Dream" with the text in front of you. If this chapter leads the reader to Elgar's music, to Newman's text, and then to personal prayer, the author will be well pleased.

There is a presence that walks the road of life with you. This presence accompanies your every moment. It shadows your every thought and feeling. On your own, or with others it is always there with you. When you were born, it came out of the womb with you, with the excitement at your arrival, and nobody noticed it. Though this presence surrounds you, you may still be blind to its companionship. The name of this presence is death.

These are the words of the Irish philosophical-theologian and poet John O'Donohue.[2] The sentiments expressed in the words initially may sound strange, but they should not be alien to the Christian. Think, for example, of St. Francis of Assisi, who speaks of death as "Sister Death." In "The Canticle of Brother Sun," Francis wrote, "Praised be You, my Lord, through our Sister Bodily Death." Of course, we do not always get on terribly well with our siblings. Sister Death may be one of the siblings we should like to keep at as far a distance as possible. But it isn't possible. A time will come, morning or evening, day or night, when each of us will have to die. The great insight of St. Francis is that death is "neither an enemy to be overcome nor a fate to be accepted but rather a friend, a kinsman, to be received with all courtesy…."[3] It is about making death a friend, strange though the language sounds. Making death a friend is of great benefit and importance. "To continually transfigure the faces of your own death ensures that at the end of your life, your physical death will be no stranger, robbing you against your will of the life that you have had; you will know its face intimately. Since you have overcome your fear, your death will be a meeting with a lifelong friend from the deepest side of your own nature."[4] This is part of what John Henry Newman was writing about in his epic poem, "The Dream of Gerontius."[5] It is his vision of what death and what happens afterward ought to be like for a Christian.

While Newman's vision in "The Dream" is enormously hopeful, as we shall see, it is not a romantic vision. He realizes all too well the ambiguity that surrounds death and dying, but equally well he refuses to concede ultimacy to that ambiguity. Newman's Gerontius moves from an understandable fear to serenity and joy. That is the way it should be, especially for a Christian. Nevertheless, one can understand this fundamental ambiguity about death and dying. On the one hand, it is the end of life as we know it in this world, the severing of relationships, business left undone. One author, speaking of the Shoah and its devastation, writes, "[Those who died in the Holocaust] were torn from mistakes they had no chance to fix; everything unfinished. All the sins of love without detail, detail without love. The regret of having spoken, of having run out of time so to speak. Of hoarding oneself. Of turning one's back too often in favour of sleep."[6] On the other hand, Christians believe that death is the portal through which we go home to the Father's house, our entry point into full communion with God.

"The Dream of Gerontius"

In 1864, Newman wrote his *Apologia pro Vita Sua*. The book is autobiographical in style and provides an account of Newman's growth and development in his spiritual and religious life. It was a turbulent period in Newman's life, and he seems to have had a vivid sense of his own impending death. This is the context in which "The Dream of Gerontius" was written. This sense of impending death reminds me of that fine poem written by the twentieth-century Welsh poet Dylan Thomas, "Do Not Go Gentle into That Good Night."

> Do not go gentle into that good night,
> Old age should burn and rave at close of day;
> Rage, rage against the dying of the light...[7]

It seems that the poem was written by Thomas in 1952 for his dying father. He watched his father grow weak and very frail with old age. Essentially he is saying to his father, "Do not let your passion for life be compromised." The line "Do not go gentle into that good night" occurs four times in this short poem, and "Rage, rage against the dying of the light" occurs three times. Whether Dylan Thomas was really speaking about his father, or about himself and his fear of death, as some critics have it, is not especially relevant for our purposes. What is relevant is the fear, and the raging against what seems to be the dying of the light of life. It is a combination of rage or anger and fear in the face of dying and death. Newman's "Gerontius" is a far cry from Dylan Thomas's advice, "Do not go gentle into that dark night." It breathes a different air.

"The Dream of Gerontius" was written over a period of three brief weeks. It was published in the periodical *The Month* in May and June 1865. Newman's method was to labor over his prose, revising and revising and revising. This text, however, seems to have sprung from deep in his soul, having taken root there over the years. A friend of Newman's, Thomas William Allies, had attended an acted performance of "The Dream" in Liverpool, at a teacher-training college, and he wrote to tell Newman about it. This is how Newman describes the writing of his poem by way of reply to Mr. Allies: "On the 17th of January last it came into my head to write it. I cannot really tell how, and I wrote on till it was finished, on small bits of paper."[8]

It describes the time, if time is indeed the right word, between dying and coming before God in judgment. It paints a picture of the ideal Christian death, with the dying man being surrounded and supported in his final agony by his friends. Newman's gift for lasting friendships is well known. However, there may be another nuance to this picture. It may be literally quite true. All around the wall near Newman's bed in the Oratory in Birmingham were pictures of his friends.

The poem is about the dying of an elderly Christian, Gerontius. The word *geron* in Greek means "an old man." The poem begins with these extraordinarily moving words:

Jesu, Maria—I am near to death,
And Thou art calling me; I know it now.
Not by the token of this faltering breath,
This chill at heart, this dampness on my brow,
(Jesu, have mercy! Mary, pray for me!)
'Tis this new feeling, never felt before,
(Be with me, Lord, in my extremity!)
That I am going, that I am no more.

Gerontius has been sick before, but this is a new feeling "never felt before." The moment of dying is described as follows:

As though my very being had given way,
As though I was no more a substance now,
And could fall back on nought to be my stay...
And drop from out the universal frame
Into that shapeless, scopeless, blank abyss,
That utter nothingness, of which I came.

Newman's description is so vivid and so intense in this passage of "The Dream" that it leads one to surmise that perhaps he had an experience, an experience of mortality, or some kind of spiritual experience, that enabled him to reach this expression in the poem. This description of emptiness is followed by the prayers of the assistants, those at his bedside, and then Gerontius makes his statement of faith:

And I hold in veneration,
    For the love of Him alone,
Holy Church, as His creation,
    And her teachings, as His own.
And I take with joy whatever
    Now besets me, pain or fear,
And with a strong will I sever
    All the ties which bind me here.

This is a powerful confession of faith that ties together his love of God and his love of the church and her teachings. He emphasizes that he "takes with joy" whatever now he is to experience. Finally, and this is very strong language, he severs "all the ties which bind [him] here." It is indeed a very powerful confession of his Christian faith. Yet, it does not save him from the terror of death. Gerontius goes on to say:

> ...for now it comes again,
> That sense of ruin, which is worse than pain,
> That masterful negation and collapse
> Of all that makes me man....

His very existence, his humanity is collapsing, is being negated, as it were, by his dying and death. He is, in his own words, "falling through the solid framework of created things." Once again, the assistants pray for Gerontius, he commends himself into the hands of the Lord like Jesus in St. Luke's Gospel—"Into thy hands I commend my spirit"—and the priest prays that wonderful prayer for the dying: "Go forth upon thy journey, Christian soul! Go from this world! Go, in the name of God...." Hearing this confident prayer, Gerontius dies. Immediately the text continues as follows:

> I went to sleep; and now I am refresh'd,
> A strange refreshment: for I feel in me
> An inexpressive lightness, and a sense
> Of freedom, as I were at length myself,
> And ne'er had been before. How still it is!

The soul of Gerontius leaves this world, and is aware of leaving this world:

> So much I know, not knowing how I know,
> That the vast universe, where I have dwelt,
> Is quitting me, or I am quitting it.

At this point, the soul feels companionship. He is not alone. His guardian angel is helping him move forward and has come to take his soul home to the house of God.

> …Someone has me fast
> Within his ample palm.…

The soul of Gerontius speaks to his guardian angel:

> Why have I now no fear at meeting [God]?
> Along my earthly life, the thought of death
> And judgment was to me most terrible.…
> Now that the hour is come, my fear is fled.…
> Now close upon me, I can forward look
> With a serenest joy.

At this point the demons come into play, demons described as having "an animal vulgarity" as they jeer at the passing of Gerontius. Whatever one makes of these demons, it may at least be claimed that they stand for the final residue of fear, doubt, and ambiguity in the face of death.

As his natural fear of dying and death is left behind, his guardian angel carries him forward toward God, and his experience is one of joy. There is no fear. Gerontius now hears "The First Choir of Angelicals" singing that marvelous hymn:

> Praise to the Holiest in the height,
>   And in the depth be praise:
> In all His words most wonderful;
>   Most sure in all His ways!

Gerontius now enters the house of judgment. The judgment, however, comes from one whose best name is Love. There is no room for fear. Once again he hears the hymn from "The Second Choir of Angelicals" and "The Third Choir of Angelicals": "Praise to the Holiest in the height." His guardian angel explains to him that these evangelical choirs "sing of thy approaching agony." What agony is being spoken of here? It is the agony of seeing the God who is Love with a simultaneous recognition that one is so unlovely.

> What then—if such thy lot—thou seest thy Judge...
> Thou wilt be sick with love, and yearn for Him....
> There is a pleading in His pensive eyes
> Will pierce thee to the quick, and trouble thee.
> And thou wilt hate and loathe thyself; for, though
> Now sinless, thou wilt feel that thou hast sinn'd,
> As never thou didst feel; and wilt desire
> To slink away, and hide thee from His sight....
> The shame of self at thought of seeing Him,—
> Will be thy veriest, sharpest purgatory.

These words immediately bring to my mind the eucharistic words of the priest-poet George Herbert in the poem "Love":

> Love bade me welcome: yet my soul drew back,
> Guilty of dust and sin.

I am unclear whether Newman was aware of this poem, but whether he was or not, the sentiments are identical. The pain of purgatory is not some external pain inflicted upon the soul. The pain of purgatory is the recognition in the presence of Love that one is not lovely. The pain of purgatory is the intense pain of regret that one has not lived a life of love.

The intensity of purgatorial regret is expressed by Newman through Gerontius in the following words spoken by the soul to his guardian angel:

> Take me away, and in the lowest deep
> There let me be,
> And there in hope the lone night-watches keep....

The soul desires to move away out of a most profound sense of utter unworthiness from the presence of the God who is Love. "Take me away....Let me be." The guardian angel who has accompanied Gerontius thus far recognizes the importance of this cleansing moment, this most intense moment of deepest regret. Gerontius feels his sinfulness. It is an immediate feeling on coming into God's loving presence. The soul is learning that

> ...the flame of Everlasting Love
> Doth burn ere it transform....

"Purgatory," as Paul McPartlan rightly has it, "is the state of grace where the process of *Christification* can be perfected."[9] It is heaven's door, not hell's threshold. Nonetheless, it takes time, as it were, to be cleansed. The angel says to the soul:

> Softly and gently, dearly-ransom'd soul,
>   In my most loving arms I now enfold thee,
> And, o'er the penal waters, as they roll,
>   I poise thee, and I lower thee, and hold thee.
>
> And carefully I dip thee in the lake....
>
> Farewell, but not forever! brother dear,
>   Be brave and patient on thy bed of sorrow;
> Swiftly shall pass thy night of trial here,
>   And I will come and wake thee on the morrow.

The guardian angel also tells the soul that it will be nursed and tended by angels during this purgatorial moment. It will not be left alone. Purgatory is described in this section of the poem almost as a mystical state. What is the time that it takes for this cleansing to occur? *Time* seems a strange word to use now that time is over for the soul who has left this life. This time of cleansing is best understood as instantaneous. Coming before the God who is nothing but unconditional Love, one comes to understand that one has been anything but unconditional love in the living of one's life. That is the moment of cleansing pain, the pain of regret, the searing pain of recognizing that one cannot return to the pilgrimage on earth to undo what one ought not to have done. Nothing could hurt more, but the hurt is the consequence of the final realization that God is Love. The passage also sounds like the Rite of Baptism: the soul is dipped into the lake of baptism, as it were, before being finalized as Body of Christ, in God.

Newman lived through the First Vatican Council (1869–70), but the Second Vatican Council (1962–65) has been called Newman's Council. The revised liturgical rites of the church that flowed from that council have, for the most part, been well received by the faithful throughout the world. If we leaf through the Rites for the Commendation of the Dying, we find a horizon of understanding that is truly Catholic, and so truly Newman's, as it were. In writing "The Dream of Gerontius" Newman reworked an ancient Latin prayer, the *Profiscere*, the first words of which are "Go forth, Christian soul." The new rite includes a formulation of this prayer. But before we get to it, we need to acknowledge the beginning of the rite. The rite says this: "One or more of the following short texts may be recited with the dying person. If necessary, they may be softly repeated two or three times." Here are some of those short scriptural texts:

"Who will separate us from the love of Christ?" (Rom 8:35)

"Whether we live or whether we die, we are the Lord's." (Rom 14:8)

"We have a building from God, a house not made with hands, eternal in the heavens." (2 Cor 5:1)

"We will be with the Lord forever." (1 Thess 4:17)

"We will see [God] as he is." (1 John 3:2)

"Even though I walk through the darkest valley, / I fear
no evil; / for you are with me." (Ps 23:4)

The rite continues with further readings from scripture and moves
into the Litany of the Saints, recalling Gerontius's prayer at the
beginning of "The Dream": "Jesu, Maria—I am near to death....
Jesu, have mercy! Mary, pray for me!" Then come the quite magnificent words of the Prayer of Commendation, words used "at the
very cusp of the divide between life and death":

Go forth, Christian soul, from this world
In the name of God the Almighty Father,
Who created you,
In the name of Jesus Christ, Son of the living God,
Who suffered for you,
In the name of the Holy Spirit,
Who was poured out upon you,
Go forth, faithful Christian.
May you live in peace this day,
May your home be with God in Zion,
With Mary, the Virgin Mother of God,
With Joseph, and all the angels and saints.

This prayer, "Go forth, Christian soul," is the gentle nudging that
may be needed to move forward from this world and to sail into
the presence of God.

After death has occurred, the ritual offers various prayers
among which the following may be found:

Saints of God, come to his/her aid!
Come to meet him/her, angels of the Lord!
Receive his/her soul and present him/her to God the
    Most High.
May Christ who called you, take you to himself;
May angels lead you to Abraham's side.

These beautiful prayers are essentially the same prayers that are reflected in Newman's poem. They indicate to us all too clearly that while there is an understandable element of fear in the unknown reality of death and dying, fear is not the final thing. Rather, a quiet hopeful confidence of coming into God's lovely presence is the final thing. This is the meaning of Newman's "Dream of Gerontius."

Sir Edward Elgar and "The Dream of Gerontius"

Why not just read the text? Why listen to the musical composition of Sir Edward Elgar? Does the music add anything to this text? I am no musician. But Newman himself said, "I always sleep better after music....Perhaps thought is music." However, I find these words of a theologian reflecting on what music does to us particularly persuasive:

> To listen seriously to music and to perform it are among our most potent ways of learning what it is to live with and before God....In this "obedience" of listening and following, we are stretched and deepened, physically challenged as performers, imaginatively as listeners. The time we have renounced, given up, is given back to us as a time in which we have become more human, more real, even (or especially) when we can't say what we have learned, only that we have changed.[10]

The claim is being made that listening seriously to music changes us. We are made different by the music. We are stretched and deepened. We are made more human. Too few things in life stretch and deepen us. Music has the capacity to do this. Being aware of the text and listening to Elgar's musical setting of "The Dream of Gerontius" seems to me a uniquely privileged moment of grace. Grace is God reaching out to us, in this case reaching out through word and music. We are changed.

Sir Edward Elgar composed the oratorio "The Dream of Gerontius" in 1900. It should be mentioned that Elgar was a Catholic and was thus inspired by his personal belief in the Catholic teaching on purgatory. He composed his oratorio for the Birmingham Music Festival, and its first performance took place in Birmingham Town Hall on October 3, 1900. Birmingham then as now is a very ordinary city, an industrial center, a city of ordinary working people. There is something entirely appropriate about the first performance of "The Dream of Gerontius" taking place in Birmingham. Birmingham Town Hall is about three miles from the Birmingham Oratory on the Hagley Road in Edgbaston, which was founded by Newman and in which he composed "The Dream." Birmingham was a far cry from the elegance of Oxford and its university. Yet it was in Birmingham that Blessed John Henry Newman lived, prayed, and worshiped, ministered to the people, and died. It was in the industrial city of Birmingham that John Henry Newman opened a church in what had been previously a gin distillery. He cared for the very ordinary people of Birmingham. When the rather pompous Msgr. George Talbot invited Newman to preach a series of Lenten sermons to his genteel English congregation in Rome, Talbot advised Newman that he "would have a more educated Audience of Protestants than could ever be the case in England." Newman replied curtly, "Birmingham people have souls, and I have neither taste nor talent for the sort of work which you cut out for me: and I beg to decline your offer." It was one of the best literary snubs in English. Arguably it was for the ordinary Christian folk that "The Dream of Gerontius" had been written. Ordinary folk can still benefit in great measure from it.

Shattering the Idols: Prayers of Petition and Intercession

Petition is profoundly a program of struggle and purification.
Deeply undertaken, it asks for the shattering of idols, that man
may be adoration.

Joseph P. Whelan[1]

I

This quote from Joseph Whelan, SJ, sets the tone for this reflection. The deepest and most appropriate posture for the person vis-à-vis God is adoration, understood as the absolute recognition of and perfect positive response to God. Adoration in this sense is eschatological, anticipated in prayerful acts of adoration in this life. As we move toward adoration, we acknowledge our utter dependence upon God through petition and intercession. As Whelan intimates, genuine petition demands the hard work of struggle and purification. This chapter explores the meaning of petitionary and intercessory prayer, not in a thoroughly systematic and analytical fashion, but simply by probing a little. The probing needs to happen because petition occurs not only in our own daily prayers but throughout the church's liturgy, from the Liturgy of the Hours to the great prayer of the Eucharist. It is human to inquire into what is going on as we make petition and intercession. Petitionary or intercessory prayer is something of a struggle and purification because it is so very easy to slip into strange, even if not, in Joseph Whelan's words, entirely "idolatrous" positions. Petition is asking benefits of God for oneself, intercession asking on behalf of another. At one level asking God for benefits flows from the command of Jesus in the Lord's Prayer, which is full of petitions. Arguably and from a purely descriptive point of view, asking God for benefits also flows from almost an innate sense of dependence on Something/ Someone greater than ourselves, which we acknowledge especially at times of vulnerability.

The question to be explored is, What does it mean to ask God for things? This takes us, in some measure, into the realm of the philosophy of religion, and this is far from clear and straightforward. There are so many competing philosophies of religion. Philosophers, like anyone who thinks, belong in a particular context, are influenced by that context both positively and negatively, and agonize toward truth. *Agon* is the Greek word for "struggle," and philosophy, we might say, is an *agonic* activity. This is how one philosopher of religion, the late Welsh philosopher Dewi Z. Phillips, puts it: "To work in the field of the philosophy of religion is like working on the Tower of Babel: one cannot take for granted that one's colleagues understand what one is saying."[2] There are different ways of doing philosophy, different traditions of thinking about religious issues, and so disagreement among different philosophers is simply a fact. Phillips may have been overstating this problem, but his witticism invites us to say clearly where we are coming from in this exploration. We are coming from the vantage point of Christian faith. We are intent upon making petition and intercession more intelligible to Christians who pray, and we hope that intelligibility may work also for those who do not make prayers of petition or intercession but are interested in how it works.

II

The first thing to note is that petition and intercession are not the only forms of prayer. "When read with sympathy, the old description does us very well: prayer is the raising of the mind and heart to God. 'Attending' might do better than 'raising.' And 'response' is more accurate yet."[3] "Raising mind and heart," "attending," "responding" all insist that reality is not self-creating, but rather is both recognition and response. Mind and heart are being raised to Something/Someone, attention and response is being given to Something/Someone. Put more personally, "I am a given." If a given, then there is a giver, or better Giver, and that is God. Because I am, there is necessarily awareness, and that awareness is prayer. Because I am gift, there is necessarily awareness, and that more intense awareness is also prayer. Prayer is all about awareness of God-who-is-Love. That awareness issues forth in adoration and praise, contrition and thanksgiving as well as petition and intercession.[4]

For Christians God is at work to turn sin and suffering to good, that is, to himself as source and *telos* (goal) of all reality. God is not an affectionate spectator on the evil and suffering of the world from the outside. He enters into creation through creating, most intensively in a unique and special way through the redemptive incarnation of the Word, our Lord Jesus Christ, so that "he takes upon himself our sin and suffering" so that "our history becomes his history." From within, God-in-Christ-through-the-Spirit transforms our self-evidently broken human condition in the direction of the most intimate communion with himself. This communion will become total and perfect at the Parousia, when "God may be all in all" (1 Cor 15:28).

St. Paul writes, "We know that all things work together for good for those who love God, who are called according to his purpose" (Rom 8:28). We do not know exactly how this happens in every single instance, but it is a fundamental conviction of Christians. It grounds and forms the basis of our understanding of all reality. This fundamental conviction flows from the axiom that "God is love..." (1 John 4:16). Everything comes from this God-who-is-Love and, at the Parousia, will return to him, perfected and made whole. That is why for St. Paul love is the greatest of the gifts (1 Cor 12—13). Love as self-donation, "the deepest etymology of love," is the motive for everything that exists on the part of God who donates-creates, and on the part of the human person who donates-responds.[5]

Thus, God is not present to reality, nor to us, as an external force among other forces. It has been superbly expressed by John H. Wright, SJ: God is present and active "in the within of all things in the universe. He is present in their within, acting to realize his purposes everywhere." Wright is not saying that God *is* the within of all things—that would be a reductive pantheism. Rather he is saying that God is *in the within* of all things.

> All things are "from him," for he is the source of the reality of all things. All things are "through him" and "in him," for he is the ultimate support of their being and activity. All things are "to him," for he is the attractive impulse, drawing them into the future, building them up through the evolutionary process into more and more complex material arrangements and, corresponding to them, more and more intense centers of inwardness or consciousness.[6]

These few sentences are powerful and invite slow, personal appropriation. God out of sheer generosity and goodness (= Love as self-donation) draws us from nothing to existence. Indeed, "God" is the answer to the question, "Why is there anything at all rather than nothing?" Or, more existentially and personally, "Why am I?" The Christian answer is "God," that is, Love (1 John 4:16). Using the words of St. Thomas Aquinas, and before him of Pseudo-Dionysius, "Goodness is diffusive of itself."[7] This is a self-authenticating principle. God creates us for communion. This is the God who evokes adoration and praise, the awareness of whom invites contrition and sorrow, whose unbounded generosity elicits thanksgiving. This is the God to whom as our source and goal we make petition and intercession.

III

There are two points of view to be ruled out in advance in this consideration of petition and intercession. The first is that nothing really happens as a result of petition, that is to say, nothing really happens in the *real world*. This viewpoint is exemplified in William James:

> If (prayer) be not effective; if it be not a give and take relation; if nothing be really transacted while it lasts; if the world is no whit different for its having taken place; then prayer, taken in this wide meaning of a sense that *something is transacting*, is of course a feeling of what is illusory, and religion must on the whole be classed, not simply as containing elements of delusion,—these undoubtedly everywhere exist,—but as being rooted in delusion altogether, just as materialists and atheists have always said it was.[8]

James is correct. If nothing is *really* happening in and through prayer, in his words if nothing is "transacting," then prayer is rooted in delusion altogether. It may be of some immediate help to the one who prays, but delusion is unhelpful in the longer run. Certainly, when religious people are in fact praying there is a real confidence, perhaps latent, perhaps inarticulate, but a real confidence that something of importance and value is in fact being "transacted," to use James's verb. There is a world of difference between one who regularly prays, and thus petitions God, and one who seldom if ever does but, in difficult circumstances, turns in prayer to God for a quick fix. Thus, Dewi Z. Phillips writes, "One might put forward a general thesis that the more tenuous the relation between the prayer and the rest of the person's life, the more suspect the prayer becomes; the likelihood of superstition increases."[9]

The second viewpoint to be ruled out in advance is the egotistical and selfish attitude that may underlie some forms of petitionary prayer. It has been well captured by the Catholic scientist Chet Raymo:

> For many people, the entire purpose of prayer is to invoke God's intervention in the course of their daily lives, to adjust the tilt of the universe in their personal favor, to redirect the stream of time ever so marginally so that benefices flow their way....I struggle to shed the shabby shawl of petitionary and formulaic prayer that I inherited as a child—to reject the default syllables "Me, Lord, Me"—so that I might attend to *things*—to swallows and auroras—to the voice that whispers in *all* of creation, to the voice that *is* all of creation.[10]

In the latter part of this passage Raymo comes close to what was meant above by God being in the within of things. Raymo evinces a strong sense of the immanence of God in creation. In the former part of the passage, however, he offers a description of petitionary prayer as egotistical and selfish: "adjusting the tilt of the universe in one's personal favor." I do not hear him denouncing petitionary prayer as such, but simply this narrow form of it. So, in our exploration of petitionary prayer, these two perspectives are a priori ruled out. We want to insist that something really happens, and to reject egotism.

So, we assume that when prayers of petition or intercession are being prayed they are being prayed from the perspective of genuine piety and devotion, not from a foxhole, not out of a superstitious set of circumstances. Let us take the difficult example, following Dewi Phillips, of parents praying when a child is dying. There is a difference between a set of parents who are in a relationship of regular awareness of and devotion to God and parents who are not. The nonreligious parents who love their child ask God to let the child live, perhaps thinking that God could save this particular child if he really wanted to, and so their role is one of trying to influence God's will. The religious parents who love their child ask God to let the child live, yes, but they understand their role as somewhat different. For them, in a relationship of regular devotion the prayer is best understood, in Phillips's words, "not as an attempt at influencing the way things go, but as an expression of, and a request for, devotion to God through the way things go." Phillips continues, "When deep religious believers pray *for* something, they are not so much asking God to bring this about, but in a way telling Him of the strength of their desires. They realize that things may not go as they wish, but they are asking to be able to go on living whatever happens. In prayers...of petition, the believer is trying to find a meaning and a hope that will deliver him from the elements in his life which threaten to destroy it...."[11] The desire for the life of the child is brought before God because it is the deep desire of the parents, but there is a fundament of trust in God whatever happens. Phillips is saying something of importance here, but it seems to me insufficient.

The fundament of trust in relationship with God remains and is primary. At the same time, however, the very act of making a genuine petition enters into the reality of the world. Each time we pray we deepen our relationship and communion with God and, therefore, the world changes because we are world, so to speak. When we ask God for things, we deepen our relationship with God. We strengthen our bond with God (petition), and we strengthen our bonds with our fellows (intercession). Both communion in and with God and communion in and with our fellows are rendered more real in prayer, and in that sense the reality of the world is changed. This is difficult to describe with any persuasive accuracy, not least because the "world" for many is what is empirically verifiable and quantifiable. The world is what is out there just now, in front of our noses. John Wright is helpful in disabusing us of this naive view of reality. He asks, "Finally, does anything ever happen that wouldn't have happened if we had not prayed?" And he responds:

> Much, all the time. For if we genuinely pray, authentically manifest a personal relationship to God in faith, then

our prayers as effective symbols enter into the order and instrumentality by which the whole of created reality is made present to God's ongoing and creative love. The world is being constantly sustained and enriched as this love reaches it through many and complex interrelationships of actions, causes, and effective symbols. Authentic prayer is one of these symbols effectively relating the world to the enriching power of God.[12]

Central to Wright's understanding of petitionary prayer is the recognition that the world is fundamentally relational. It is a web of relationality. In such an understanding of the world, prayer as a human act enters into this web of relationality and, therefore, makes a difference. "Prayer is the act of bringing our moment-by-moment connectedness to God into our consciousness," and in this bringing to consciousness the web of relationality in which we live is affected, is changed, even if that may not be measured by some empirical means.[13]

IV

The acknowledgment of a relational world takes us to the contribution of Marjorie Hewitt Suchocki (born in 1933), a Methodist and a process theologian. She is one of the few process theologians who have given attention to prayer and especially to petitionary prayer. Her insights illuminate this exploration of petitionary prayer.

Of course, one does not need to subscribe to process theology in order to qualify or perhaps even reject elements of the God of classical theism. A good example is the late John Macquarrie (1919–2007). In his personal devotional life Macquarrie was in many ways quite traditional, even as he was adamant that classical theism was no longer helpful.[14] Macquarrie was an immensely influential systematic theologian, but many who are not professionally involved in teaching theology but are committed

Christians share his sentiments. In this regard Hubert Richards, a popular scripture scholar, offers a thumbnail sketch of this God of classical theism and follows it up with an anecdote: "All that exists is totally related to [God]. But he is in no way related to his creatures. Indeed he is the Eternally Self-Sufficient, existing of and by himself. Is it any wonder that ordinary people would prefer such a God to keep his distance? They understand hardly anything about him, and what they do understand does not attract them." Here is Richards's anecdote:

> I was lecturing on this topic to an audience of priests, and in the discussion one of them took exception to my remarks. I was trivializing the God of Christian traditional theology, who was in reality a most exciting object of contemplation. He proceeded to enlarge upon this, but had to stop short after two or three sentences: most of his audience had switched off and were talking to each other. Even the professionals are no longer interested in the God of the scholars.[15]

Richards is not espousing process theology but describing what I think is a very widespread viewpoint today. Aspects of the God of classical theism are rejected by many today. I do not intend an *apologia* for process theology as such, but rather wish to use the rich thought of Marjorie Suchocki to open up some further perspectives on petitionary prayer.

Without going into the details of a Christian process theology, let us acknowledge the starting point: "In God, the many are one everlastingly, each contributing to the others and receiving from the others in the unity of God."[16] This sentence of Suchocki's draws together, at least implicitly, Wright's point that God is in the within of everything and that reality is a web of relationality. As an action, prayer occurs within this web of relationality and makes a difference. Her basic premise is that what God can do is reality based and not magically based, that "God has an effect upon how and what this universe is and is becoming, and that this universe has a return effect upon God."[17] Human beings live within a complex nexus of relationships, continuously affected by what is other than themselves. This does not lead to total determinism because we have a degree of freedom to respond. "Relationships create an ongoing dance of influence, response, and influence once again, and in the process, we develop and express our own characters."[18] Just as we respond to a complex nexus of relationships, and our character is expressed through our responses, something similar is true of God. There is, however, an important difference: "There would be nothing to which God did not relate." So, if God relates and responds to everything, "all things and all persons eventually meet in God through God's feelings of them and for them."[19] The expression she uses sounds a little strange—indeed, it is the strangeness of the language that is one of the impediments to the reception of process theological categories—but it is worth staying the course.

"Praying for another's well-being allows God to weave us into that other's well-being. In this manner we become part of those for whom we pray, and they become part of us. All things relate to all other things." Our conscious awareness of this necessary relationality is always limited, and, indeed, it may go for the most part entirely unnoticed by us. That does not mean that relationality is not real. The reality of relationality means that we are connected with everyone and ultimately with everything. "Praying lifts [the] loose connections to our conscious awareness in the context of God's presence." Prayer weaves everyone and everything together, so that we participate in one another's work, so that we strengthen one another, through the grace and power of God. Thus, "Prayer changes the 'isness' of the world."[20] That is a particularly fine phrase: "Prayer changes the 'isness' of the world." Notice that Suchocki is not claiming that prayer changes the "isness" of the world necessarily in the direction of how we should like it to be. Rather, she is affirming that if the world is constituted by relationality in this thoroughgoing manner, prayer is part of this relational reality that is the world. Prayer, therefore, changes the "isness" of that relational world.

Let us go back to the earlier example of praying that a loved one who is dying might live. How does Suchocki's theological perspective interpret this heart-rending pain? Immediately, she recognizes the fundamental horizon within which all prayer for healing occurs, the horizon of death: "The fact is that the context for prayers of healing is our mortality. We will all die; it is not a question of if, but a question of when."[21] Alongside this self-evident reality of our mortality lies the less self-evident reality of God. For Suchocki, "God works with the world as it is in order to bring it to where it can be." If that sounds a little abstract, she uses a fertile image to convey the meaning: "Imagine that the God of the universe, like flowing water, is in intimate relation with all elements throughout the universe, and therefore with all our earth as well. Imagine that God, in creative relation to the earth, woos the earth so that it becomes a world, and woos the world in the hope that it might yet become a peaceful and just reflection of the divine image."[22] The image of water helps us come to terms with the primary metaphysical notion of God's being in the within of reality. Not only, however, is God present—God is also active. Water as the primary symbol of life stands for God bringing life into being and luring life to a greater plenitude of life.

Now back to our difficult case of a loved one who is dying, but from this believing philosophical backdrop. Suchocki maintains that where reversibility of illness is still possible, prayers for the healing of the child would be important. "God can use our prayers to bring healing about." If, however, irreversibility of the illness has come about, prayer for healing should still continue because "healing comes in many forms, and there is a health that is deeper than death."[23] For a Christian, healing is not a synonym for continued time on earth. She provides a moving example from her own experience, the example of her mother's dying and death. Read it in her own words:

The forms of healing, I learned, are not only physical. At one point my mother, who had been in a semi-coma, roused herself and miraculously lifted her head and upper body from the bed, stretching out her arms toward us, her grown children. My brothers took her arms; I, at the foot of the bed, touched her feet. She looked at me and said, "Do you want to join me? It's affirming." At first I inwardly cringed—to join her in death! No! But in the instant I knew she was right. We *had* each other joined her, through our deep love and our prayers that so united us with her, and it *was* affirming. We were touching the profound places of the human spirit in that hospital room, and discovering that the process of dying was holy. Then she looked at us all and said, "My heart is filled with overwhelming love." I knew then that my prayers were answered, and my mother died a healthy woman. There is a health that is deeper than death.[24]

Prayer changes the "isness" of the world. The process theological perspective insists constantly that God works with the world as it is to where it can be. Where it can be is always "in the direction of deeper and richer modes of human community," and Suchocki's mother was moving into that deeper and richer mode of community, participating fully and finally in the Community that is Father-Son-Spirit. Prayers for those who are terminally ill are important because they can work: "a health that is deeper than death. And underneath are the everlasting arms."[25]

Something similar emerges for Hubert Richards. He raises a series of questions that intentionally coincide with Suchocki's understanding. "Could it be that there is some other purpose in praying, distinct from having the prayer answered by an outside agency? Are we urged to continue praying for things, even against impossible odds, even when we know they will not and cannot be granted, because the very act of praying is able to achieve things which simply would not be achieved if people did not pray?"[26] The affirming context of Suchocki's mother's death, the discovery that the difficult process of dying was holy, came about through the very act of praying. Prayer changes the "isness" of the world.

Both Suchocki and Richards note the importance of praying for our enemies. Suchocki writes, "How we are makes a difference in how that other can be, and how the other is makes a difference in how we can be, for God works with the world as it is in order to lead it to where it can be."[27] So, in Suchocki's terms, praying for the one who has offended us and praying for the offender's well-being can increase our own well-being. This must be so because the world is a web of interrelationality. "To continue in hatred is to block the transforming power of God that can lead us even through this tragic condition." Only God can know the fullness of circumstances, so that when prayer is made for an enemy, an offender, or one who has injured us, the prayer is released to God so that God may do what may be done.[28] Richards writes, "It is by definition impossible to continue in a state of enmity towards those whom one forgives." And he adds pointedly that "the mere act of praying has radically altered the situation."[29] Prayer changes the "isness" of the world.

Conclusion

Some may feel that these few inchoate thoughts on prayer have had the effect of excluding God from the scene altogether. This returns us to the opening words, that prayer "shatters the idols." The reflections offered here certainly move us away from sheerly inadequate views of God, distant and remote from the world, intervening on behalf of some and not of others. This little chapter has solved no philosophical problems about the prayer of petition and intercession. Its purpose was very simply to provide "some thoughts" in concert with some contemporary thinkers, to move beyond trying to tilt the universe in our personal favor. If the chapter assists in achieving this modest goal, that is enough. However, far more important than thinking about prayer is doing it.

Notes

Introduction

1. Kevin W. Irwin, "Authentic Worship in Spirit and in Truth," *Pastoral Music*, October 2008, p. 51.

2. Aidan Kavanagh, OSB, *On Liturgical Theology* (New York: Pueblo, 1984), pp. 113–14.

Chapter 1: The Liturgical Trinity

1. Andrew Louth, *Discerning the Mystery* (Oxford: Clarendon Press, 1983), p. 71.

2. Michael Paul Gallagher, SJ, "Praying: Ringing in the Changes," *Furrow* 39 (1988): 690.

3. David F. Ford, *The Future of Christian Theology* (Oxford and Chichester: Blackwell-Wiley, 2011), p. 20.

4. Hans Urs von Balthasar, *The Grain of Wheat* (San Francisco: Ignatius Press, 1995), p. 12.

5. British Council of Churches, *The Forgotten Trinity* (London: British Council of Churches, 1989), p. 13.

6. Walter Kasper, *The God of Jesus Christ* (London: SCM, 1983), pp. 245–46.

7. Hippolytus, *The Apostolic Tradition*, 21.15ff, translation adapted from Bernard Botte, *Hippolyte de Rome: la tradition apostolique*, 2nd ed. (Paris: Editions du Cerf, 1984), pp. 85–87.

8. Translation adapted from Peter Holmes, *Adversus Praxean* (26:11), *The Writings of Tertullian*, Vol. II. Ante-Nicene Christian Library (Edinburgh: T. and T. Clark, 1870), p. 395.

9. Justin Martyr, *Apology I.65*, cited in *Prayers of the Eucharist: Early and Reformed*, 3rd ed., ed. Ronald C. D. Jasper and Geoffrey J. Cuming (New York: Pueblo, 1987), p. 28.

10. Cited in Jasper and Cuming, *Prayers of the Eucharist*, p. 35.

11. Catherine LaCugna provides a good outline in her essay "Trinity and Liturgy," in *The New Dictionary of Sacramental Worship*, ed. Peter E. Fink, SJ (Collegeville, MN: Liturgical Press, 1990), p. 1294.

12. Raymond Moloney, SJ, *The Eucharistic Prayers in Worship, Preaching and Study* (Dublin: Dominican Publications, 1985), pp. 59–60.

13. Enrico Mazza, *The Eucharistic Prayers of the Roman Rite* (New York: Pueblo, 1986), p. 187. See also Moloney, *The Eucharistic Prayers in Worship, Preaching and Study*, p. 61.

14 Geoffrey Wainwright, "The Ecumenical Rediscovery of the Trinity," *One in Christ* 34 (1998): 95–124. See also Wainwright's fine essay in his *Worship with One Accord: Where Liturgy and Ecumenism Embrace* (New York and Oxford, UK: Oxford University Press, 1997), pp. 237–50.

15. Wainwright, "The Ecumenical Rediscovery of the Trinity," p. 110.

16. Ibid., pp. 111–12.

17. Geoffrey Preston, OP, *Hallowing the Time* (New York / Ramsey, NJ: Paulist Press, 1980), p. 155.

18. The homilies of Walter Burghardt, SJ, published by Paulist Press, are well known and easily accessible. For Preston, as well as *Hallowing the Time*, one might wish to consult his excellent *Faces of the Church* (Edinburgh: T. and T. Clark, 1997), especially at pp. 261–98.

Chapter 2: Worship and the Catholic Imagination

1. Fergus Kerr, OP, *Theology after Wittgenstein* (Oxford, UK: Blackwell, 1986), pp. 183–84.

2. Ninian Smart, *The Religious Experience of Mankind* (New York: Scribner's, 1969), p. 16. The book has gone through a number of revisions, including the title. Reference here is to this first edition. Smart took his understanding of worship further in his *The Concept of Worship* (London: Macmillan, 1972).

3. Robert Barron, *Heaven in Stone and Glass* (New York: Crossroad, 2000), p. 49.

4. Margaret Visser, *The Geometry of Love* (New York: North Point, 2000), pp. 11–12.

5. Jean Corbon, OP, *The Wellspring of Worship* (New York / Mahwah, NJ: Paulist Press, 1988), p. 132.

6. M. Francis Mannion, *Masterworks of God: Essays in Liturgical Theory and Practice* (Chicago/Mundelein, IL: Hillenbrand Books/Liturgy Training Publications, 2004), pp. 145–46.

7. Ibid., p. 147.

8. Visser, *The Geometry of Love*, pp. 14–15, 126–27.

9. Corbon, *The Wellspring of Worship*, p. 79.

10. Barron, *Heaven in Stone and Glass*, 51.

11. Ibid., pp. 107, 121.

12. Ibid., p. 52.

13. Homily on Luke 23:8.

14. Barron, *Heaven in Stone and Glass*, p. 51.

15. Andrew Greeley, *The Catholic Imagination* (Berkeley-Los Angeles-London: University of California Press, 2000), p. 1.

16. Ibid., pp. 77–78.

17. Visser, *The Geometry of Love*, p. 62.

18. Ibid.

19. Corbon, *The Wellspring of Worship*, p. 131.

20. Ibid., p. 105.

21. Ibid., pp. 115–16.

22. Ibid., p. 118.
23. Ibid., p. 137.
24. Ibid., p. 138.
25. Ibid.

Chapter 3: The Holy Scriptures

1. Alexander Schmemann, *The Eucharist* (Crestwood, NY: St. Vladimir's Seminary Press, 1988), p. 68.
2. Carlo M. Martini, SJ, "The School of the Word," *Worship* 61 (1987): 194.
3. See Raymond Moloney, *Our Splendid Eucharist* (Dublin: Veritas, 2003), pp. 22–23.
4. Mark McIntosh, *Mystical Theology* (Oxford, UK: Blackwell, 1998), p. 43.
5. Vatican II, Constitution on the Sacred Liturgy (*Sacrosanctum Concilium*), no. 7, accessible at http://www.vatican.va/archive/hist_councils/ii_vatican_council/documents/vat-ii_const_19631204_sacrosanctum-concilium_en.html.
6. Vatican II, Constitution on Divine Revelation (*Dei Verbum*), no. 21, accessible at http://www.vatican.va/archive/hist_councils/ii_vatican_council/documents/vat-ii_const_19651118_dei-verbum_en.html.
7. Norman P. Tanner, SJ, ed., *Decrees of the Ecumenical Councils*, Vol. II (London and Washington, DC: Sheed and Ward and Georgetown University Press, 1990), pp. 693–94.
8. Moloney, *Our Splendid Eucharist*, p. 21.
9. Ibid., p. 145.

Chapter 4: Preachers on Preaching

1. Rowan D. Williams, "The Sermon," in *Living the Eucharist*, ed. Stephen Conway (London: Darton, Longman and Todd, 2001), p. 47.

2. For an appreciation of Msgr. Crichton see Owen F. Cummings, "James Dunlop Crichton (1907–2001)," *Antiphon* 6 (2001): 8–11.

3. Peter Gomes, "Preaching as a Matter of Trust: Recovering the Nerve of the Pulpit," in *Theology in the Service of the Church*, ed. Wallace M. Alston Jr. (Grand Rapids: Eerdmans, 2000), p. 100.

4. Ibid., pp. 104–5.

5. P. Glorieux, "Alan of Lille," *New Catholic Encyclopedia*, Vol. 1 (Washington, DC: Catholic University of America, 1967), p. 239.

6. Gillian R. Evans, "Alan of Lille," in *Concise Encyclopedia of Preaching*, ed. William H. Willimon and Richard Lischer (Louisville: Westminster John Knox, 1995), p. 9.

7. *Alan of Lille: The Art of Preaching*, trans. with an introduction by Gillian R. Evans (Kalamazoo, MI: Cistercian Publications, 1981), p. 6.

8. Evans, "Alan of Lille," p. 10.

9. Gillian R. Evans, *Philosophy and Theology in the Middle Ages* (London: Routledge, 1993), p. 14.

10. The citations in this section are taken from chapter 1, "On Preaching," in *Alan of Lille: The Art of Preaching*, pp. 16–22.

11. Cited in Gillian R. Evans, *Alan of Lille: The Frontiers of Theology in the Later Twelfth Century* (Cambridge, UK: Cambridge University Press, 1983), p. 59.

12. Louis Bouyer, *Orthodox Spirituality and Protestant and Anglican Spirituality* (London: Burns and Oates, 1965), p. 125.

13. Ibid.

14. David F. Ford, "George Herbert: The Centrality of God," *Theology* 96 (1992): 360. For this tradition of Anglican theology in poetry see L. William Countryman, *The Poetic Imagination: An Anglican Spiritual Tradition* (Maryknoll, NY: Orbis, 1999). For an introduction to Herbert's liturgical and eucharistic theology see Owen F. Cummings, *Eucharistic Doctors* (New York / Mahwah, NJ: Paulist Press, 2005), pp. 195–202.

15. Ann P. Slater, ed., *George Herbert: The Complete English Works* (London: David Campbell, 1995), pp. 195–254.

16. Ibid., pp. 64–65. See Richard Strier, *Love Known: Theology and Experience in George Herbert's Poetry* (Chicago and London: University of Chicago Press, 1983), pp. 128–29.

17. William Barclay, *A Spiritual Autobiography* (Grand Rapids: Eerdmans, 1975), p. 72.

18. Some helpful remarks on and illustrations from Barclay's own preaching may be found in Clive L. Rawlins, *William Barclay: The Authorized Biography* (Grand Rapids: Eerdmans, 1984), pp. 179–84, 324–29.

19. The citations in what follows are drawn from *A Spiritual Autobiography*, pp. 74–98.

20. Peter Gomes, "Preaching as a Matter of Trust," p. 100.

Chapter 5: The Eucharist

1. *Summa Theologiae* 3a.73.3.

2. Raymond Moloney, SJ, "The Doctrine on the Eucharist," in *Commentary on the Catechism of the Catholic Church*, ed. Michael J. Walsh (Collegeville, MN: Liturgical Press, 1994), p. 260.

3. Ibid., pp. 260–61.

4. Pope Benedict XVI comments briefly on this issue in his recent book *Jesus of Nazareth, Part Two: Holy Week* (San Francisco: Ignatius Press, 2011).

5. Moloney, "The Doctrine on the Eucharist," p. 262.

6. Ibid.

7. Robert Sokolowski, "Steps into the Eucharist: The Phenomenology of the Mass," *Crisis* #12 (September 1994): 18.

8. Aidan Nichols, OP, *The Service of Glory* (Edinburgh: T. and T. Clark, 1997), pp. 59–60.

9. Moloney, "The Doctrine on the Eucharist," p. 266.

10. Ibid., 268. See the similar and beautifully expressed sentiments of Max Thurian, "The Liturgy and Contemplation," *Antiphon* 1 (1996): 2–6, especially 5.

11. Moloney, "The Doctrine on the Eucharist," p. 268.

12. Ibid.

Chapter 6: Eucharistic Theology

1. Aidan Nichols, OP, *The Holy Eucharist* (Dublin: Veritas, 1991), p. 102.

2. Ernest Graf, OSB, "Abbot Anscar Vonier," *In Memoriam Abbot Vonier* (Buckfast, UK: Buckfast Abbey Chronicle, 1939), p. 26.

3. Abbot Wilfrid Upson, OSB, "Abbot Anscar Vonier," *In Memoriam Abbot Vonier*, p. 3.

4. Ernest Graf, OSB, *Abbot Vonier* (Westminster, MD: Newman Press, 1957), p. 92.

5. Aidan Nichols, OP, *Dominican Gallery: Portrait of a Culture* (Leominster, UK: Fowler Wright Books, 1997), p. 386.

6. Ibid., p. 387.

7. Eric L. Mascall, *Corpus Christi* (London-New York-Toronto: Longmans, Green and Co., 1953), p. 94. For an appreciation of Mascall's contribution to eucharistic theology, see the chapter on Mascall in Owen F. Cummings, *Canterbury Cousins: Contemporary Anglican Eucharistic Theology* (New York / Mahwah, NJ: Paulist Press, 2007).

8. Colman O'Neill, OP, *Sacramental Realism* (Wilmington, DE: Michael Glazier, 1983), p. 103.

9. Anscar Vonier, *A Key to the Doctrine of the Eucharist* (Westminster, MD: Newman Press, 1951), p. vii. The original date of publication was 1925.

10. Ibid., p. 36.

11. Ibid., p. 27.

12. Ibid., p. 32.

13. Ibid., p. 20.

14. Ibid., p. 41.

15. Ibid., p. 45.

16. Ibid., p. 14.

17. (London: Sheed and Ward, 1963).

18. Vonier, *A Key to the Doctrine of the Eucharist*, pp. 66–67.

19. Ibid., p. 194.

20. Dom John Chapman, OSB, review of *A Key to the Doctrine of the Eucharist*, in *Downside Review* 44 (1926): 95.

21. Ibid., p. 96.

22. Vonier, *A Key to the Doctrine of the Eucharist*, p. 145.

23. Ibid., p. 150.

24. Raymond Moloney, SJ, *The Eucharist* (Collegeville, MN: Liturgical Press, 1995), p. 179.

25. Vonier, *A Key to the Doctrine of the Eucharist*, p. 89.

26. Oliver C. Quick, *The Christian Sacraments* (London: Nisbet, 1927), p. 242. For an account of Quick's own eucharistic theology, see Cummings, *Canterbury Cousins.*

27. Liam Walsh, OP, *The Sacraments of Initiation* (London: Geoffrey Chapman, 1988), p. 257. See also Edward J. Kilmartin, SJ, *The Eucharist in the West: History and Theology* (Collegeville, MN: Liturgical Press, 1998), pp. 252–54.

28. Vonier, *A Key to the Doctrine of the Eucharist*, p. 178.

29. Ibid., p. 181.

30. Joseph Neuner and Jacques Dupuis, eds., *The Christian Faith in the Doctrinal Documents of the Catholic Church*, rev. ed. (London: Collins, 1983), p. 416.

31. Vonier, *A Key to the Doctrine of the Eucharist*, p. 258.

32. Ibid., p. 260.

33. Chapman, review of *A Key to the Doctrine of the Eucharist*, p. 98.

Chapter 7: Eucharist as Life

1. Raymond Moloney, SJ, *Our Splendid Eucharist* (Dublin: Veritas, 2003), p. 37.

2. John F. Baldovin, SJ, *Bread of Life, Cup of Salvation* (Lanham, MD: Rowman and Littlefield, 2003), p. 2.

3. George Pattison, *The End of Theology and the Task of Thinking about God* (London: SCM, 1998), pp. 44–45.

4. L. William Countryman, *Forgiven and Forgiving* (Harrisburg: Morehouse, 1998), p. 83.

5. Kenneth Burke, *The Philosophy of Literary Form*, 3rd ed. (Berkeley: University of California Press, 1973), pp. 110–11.

6. Timothy Radcliffe, OP, *Sing a New Song: The Christian Vocation* (Springfield, IL: Templegate, 1999), p. 249.

7. Jeremy Driscoll, OSB, *What Happens at Mass* (Chicago: Liturgy Training Publications, 2005), p. 64.

8. Baldovin, *Bread of Life*, p. 63.

9. Driscoll, *What Happens at Mass*, p. 10.

10. Robert Barron, *The Strangest Way: Walking the Christian Path* (Maryknoll, NY: Orbis, 2002), p. 160.

11. Aidan Nichols, OP, *The Service of Glory: The Catechism of the Catholic Church on Worship, Ethics, Spirituality* (Edinburgh: T. & T. Clark, 1997), p. 57.

12. Barron, *The Strangest Way*, p. 161.

13. Louis Bouyer, *Liturgical Piety* (Notre Dame, IN: University of Notre Dame Press, 1955), p. 257.

14. Timothy Radcliffe, OP, *I Call You Friends* (New York and London: Continuum, 2001), p. 20.

Chapter 8: The Eucharist as Theodicy

1. Frances M. Young, "Suffering," in *The Oxford Companion to Christian Thought*, ed. Adrian Hastings et al. (New York and Oxford, UK: Oxford University Press, 2000), p. 689.

2. See Frances M. Young, *Face to Face* (London: Epworth, 1986).

3. See John Thiel, *God, Evil and Innocent Suffering* (New York: Crossroad, 2000); Terrence W. Tilley, *Evils of Theodicy* (Washington, DC: Georgetown University Press, 1991); Kenneth Surin, *Theology and the Problem of Evil* (Oxford, UK: Blackwell, 1986).

4. Paul G. Crowley, SJ, *Unwanted Wisdom: Suffering, the Cross and Hope* (New York: Continuum, 2005), pp. 78–79.

5. Margaret Spufford, *Celebration: A Story of Suffering and Joy* (London: Mowbray, 1989).

6. Ibid., p. 123.

7. Ibid., p. 21.

8. Ibid., pp. 28–29.

9. The term *theodicy* was coined by Gottfried Wilhelm Leibniz, *Theodicy* (1710) to denote an attempt to demonstrate that this world is the best possible world that God could have created.

10. Spufford, *Celebration*, p. 73.

11. Ibid., p. 80.

12. From an unpublished sermon preached by Professor Margaret Spufford at St. Edward's Church, Cambridge, Passion Sunday, 2005, available online.

13. Spufford, *Celebration*, p. 20.

14. Jeremy Driscoll, OSB, "Adoration of the Blessed Sacrament," in *A Book of Readings on the Eucharist* (Washington, DC: National Conference of Catholic Bishops, 2000), p. 80.

15. John D. Laurance, SJ, "The Eucharist and Eucharistic Adoration," *Louvain Studies* 26 (2001): 330.

16. Karl Rahner, SJ, "Eucharistic Worship," in his *Theological Investigations*, Vol. 23 (New York: Crossroad, 1992), p. 116.

17. Spufford, *Celebration*, pp. 89–90.

18. Ibid., 85–86.

19. Karl Rahner, SJ, "The Eucharist and Suffering," in his *Theological Investigations*, Vol. 3 (New York: Seabury, 1974), pp. 161–70.

Chapter 9: Benediction

1. J. R. R. Tolkien to his young son, Michael, March 1941, cited in *Letters of J. R. R. Tolkien*, ed. Humphrey Carpenter (Boston: Houghton Mifflin, 1981), p. 340.

2. Karl Rahner, SJ, "Eucharistic Worship," in his *Theological Investigations*, Vol. 23 (New York: Crossroad, 1992), p. 116.

3. Mark Searle, "Benediction," in *Encyclopedia of Catholicism*, ed. Richard P. McBrien (San Francisco: HarperCollins, 1995), p. 155.

4. V. L. Kennedy, CSB, "The Moment of Consecration and the Elevation of the Host," *Medieval Studies* 6 (1944): 121–50, especially 122, 148–50.

5. Searle, "Benediction," p. 155.

6. Maur Burbach, OSB, "Benediction of the Blessed Sacrament," *New Catholic Encyclopedia*, Vol. 2 (Washington, DC: Catholic University of America, 1967), p. 304.

7. Nathan Mitchell, OSB, *Cult and Controversy: The Worship of the Eucharist outside Mass* (New York: Pueblo, 1982), p. 205.

8. Brian McNeil, CRV, *The Master Is Here: Biblical Reflections on Eucharistic Adoration* (Dublin: Veritas, 1997), p. 5.

9. Mitchell, *Cult and Controversy*, p. 206.

10. Ibid., pp. 207–8.

11. *Holy Communion and Worship of the Eucharist outside Mass* (New York: Catholic Camp Book Company, 1976), no. 5.

12. Ibid., no. 79.

13. For a sense of Macquarrie's contribution to theology, see Owen F. Cummings, *John Macquarrie: A Master of Theology* (New York / Mahwah, NJ: Paulist Press, 2002), and at much greater length and fuller consideration *The Theology of John Macquarrie: A Comprehensive and Contextual Exploration* (Lampeter, UK, and Lewiston, NY: Edwin Mellen, 2010).

14. John Macquarrie, *Paths in Spirituality*, 2nd ed. (Harrisburg: Morehouse, 1992), p. 107. The original edition was published in 1972.

15. Ibid., p. 107.

16. Ibid., pp. 108–9.

17. Cathal Daly, "Eucharistic Devotion," in *Understanding the Eucharist*, ed. Patrick McGoldrick (Dublin: Gill and Macmillan, 1969), p. 91.

18. Ibid., p. 93.

19. *Holy Communion and Worship of the Eucharist outside Mass*, nos. 95–96.

20. Macquarrie, *Paths in Spirituality*, p. 112.

21. Ibid., p. 113.

22. According to the count of Joachim Becker, "The Heart in the Language of the Bible," in *Faith in Christ and the Worship of Christ*, ed. Leo Scheffczyk (San Francisco: Ignatius Press, 1986), p. 24.

23. Ibid., p. 27.

24. John Macquarrie, *A Guide to the Sacraments* (New York: Continuum, 1997), p. 153.

Chapter 10: Reconciliation

1. David F. Ford, *The Shape of Living* (London: HarperCollins, 1997), p. 14.

2. Robert Barron, *The Strangest Way: Walking the Christian Path* (Maryknoll, NY: Orbis, 2002), p. 100.

3. Regis A. Duffy, OFM, "Reconciliation," in *The New Dictionary of Theology*, ed. J. A. Komonchak, M. Collins, and D. A. Lane (Collegeville, MN: Liturgical Press, 1987), p. 830.

4. Joseph A. Favazza, "The Eucharistic Table, a Reconciling Table? Our Belief, Our Experience, Our Dilemma," in *The Many Presences of Christ*, ed. Timothy Fitzgerald and David A. Lysik (Chicago: Liturgy Training Publications, 1999), p. 88.

5. Archbishop Desmond Tutu, *No Future without Forgiveness* (London: Rider, 1999), cited in the fine review of Bruce Botha, SJ, in *The Month*, January 2001, p. 43.

6. Botha, review of *No Future without Forgiveness*, p. 43.

7. James P. Mackey, *Jesus the Man and the Myth* (New York / Ramsey, NJ: Paulist Press, 1979), p. 137.

8. Nuala O'Faolain, *My Dream of You* (New York: Riverhead, 2001).

9. Anne Tyler, *Saint Maybe* (New York: Knopf, 1991).

10. O'Faolain, *My Dream of You*, p. 21.

11. Ibid., p. 23.

12. Ibid., p. 526.

13. Paul Bail, *Anne Tyler: A Critical Companion* (Westport, CT: Greenwood, 1998), p. 155.

14. Tyler, *Saint Maybe*, pp. 123–24.

15. L. Gregory Jones, "The Craft of Forgiveness," *Theology Today* 50 (1993): 350.

16. Bail, *Anne Tyler*, p. 165.

17. From George Herbert's poem "Discipline."

18. L. Gregory Jones, *Embodying Forgiveness: A Theological Analysis* (Grand Rapids: Eerdmans, 1995), p. 297. See also Stanley Hauerwas, *Dispatches from the Front* (Durham, NC, and London: Duke University Press, 1994), pp. 80–88.

Chapter 11: Death and God's Lovely Presence

1. Henry Tristram, ed., *John Henry Newman: Autobiographical Writings* (New York: Sheed and Ward, 1957), p. 268.

2. John O'Donohue, *Anam Chara* (New York: Harper-Collins, 1997), p. 187.

3. Noel Dermot O'Donoghue, ODC, *The Holy Mountain: Approaches to the Mystery of Prayer* (Wilmington, DE: Michael Glazier, 1983), p. 142.

4. O'Donohue, *Anam Chara*, p. 187.

5. The text of "The Dream of Gerontius" is public domain and is available in a wide variety of sources.

6. Anne Michaels, *Fugitive Pieces* (London: Bloomsbury, 1998), p. 147.

7. In *Inventions of Farewell: A Book of Elegies*, ed. Sandra M. Gilbert (New York and London: Norton, 2001), p. 47.

8. Tristam, in *The Dream of Gerontius*, ed. Gregory Winterton (London and Oxford: Mowbray, 1986), p. xviii.

9. Paul McPartlan, "Go Forth, Christian Soul," *One in Christ* 34 (1998): 248.

10. Rowan Williams, *Open to Judgment: Sermons and Addresses* (London: Darton, Longman and Todd, 1994), p. 248.

Chapter 12: Shattering the Idols

1. Joseph P. Whelan, SJ, *Benjamin: Essays in Prayer* (New York-Paramus-Toronto: Newman Press, 1972), p. 65.

2. Dewi Z. Phillips, *The Concept of Prayer* (New York: Seabury, 1981), p. 1.

3. Whelan, *Benjamin*, p. 50.

4. See Owen F. Cummings, *Thinking about Prayer* (Eugene, OR: Wipf and Stock, 2009), pp. 1–12.

5. Whelan, *Benjamin*, pp. 11, 30.

6. John H. Wright, SJ, *A Theology of Christian Prayer* (New York: Pueblo, 1979), pp. 45–49.

7. Aquinas, *Summa Theologiae*, Ia.27.5; Pseudo-Dionysius, *On the Divine Names*, IV.20.

8. William James, *The Varieties of Religious Experience* (London: Longmans Green, 1941), p. 465.

9. Phillips, *The Concept of Prayer*, p. 115.

10. Chet Raymo, *Climbing Brandon: Science and Faith on Ireland's Holy Mountain* (New York: Walker and Co., 2004), pp. 157, 167.

11. Phillips, *The Concept of Prayer*, p. 121.

12. Wright, *A Theology of Christian Prayer*, p. 81.

13. Marjorie Suchocki, *In God's Presence: Theological Reflections on Prayer* (St. Louis, MO: Chalice, 1996), p. 33.

14. See Owen F. Cummings, *The Theology of John Macquarrie: A Comprehensive and Contextual Exploration* (Lewiston, NY: Edwin Mellen, 2010).

15. Hubert J. Richards, *What Happens When You Pray?* (London: SCM, 1980), p. 33.

16. Marjorie H. Suchocki, *God-Christ-Church*, rev. ed. (New York: Crossroad, 1989), pp. 217–18.

17. Suchocki, *In God's Presence*, p. 43.

18. Ibid., p. 44.

19. Ibid., pp. 44–45.

20. Ibid., pp. 47–49.

21. Ibid., p. 58.

22. Ibid., p. 19.
23. Ibid., pp. 59–60.
24. Ibid., p. 61.
25. Ibid., p. 62.
26. Richards, *What Happens When You Pray?*, p. 61.
27. Suchocki, *In God's Presence*, p. 53.
28. Ibid., pp. 54–55.
29. Richards, *What Happens When You Pray?*, pp. 63–64.

Bibliography

Bail, Paul. *Anne Tyler: A Critical Companion.* Westport, CT: Greenwood, 1998.

Baldovin, John F., SJ. *Bread of Life, Cup of Salvation.* Lanham, MD: Rowman and Littlefield, 2003.

Balthasar, Hans Urs von. *The Grain of Wheat.* San Francisco: Ignatius Press, 1995.

Barclay, William. *A Spiritual Biography.* Grand Rapids: Eerdmans, 1975.

Barron, Robert. *Heaven in Stone and Glass.* New York: Crossroad, 2000.

———. *The Strangest Way: Walking the Christian Path.* Maryknoll, NY: Orbis, 2002.

Becker, Joachim. "The Heart in the Language of the Bible." In *Faith in Christ and the Worship of Christ,* edited by Leo Scheffczyk. San Francisco: Ignatius Press, 1986.

Botha, Bruce, SJ. Review: Desmond Tutu, *No Future without Forgiveness.* London: Rider, 1999. *The Month* (January 2001): 43.

Botte, Bernard, OSB. *Hippolyte de Rome: la tradition apostolique.* 2nd rev. ed. Paris: Editions du Cerf, 1984.

Bouyer, Louis. *Liturgical Piety.* Notre Dame, IN: University of Notre Dame Press, 1955.

———. *Orthodox Spirituality and Protestant and Anglican Spirituality.* London: Burns and Oates, 1965.

British Council of Churches. *The Forgotten Trinity.* London: British Council of Churches, 1989.

Burbach, Maur, OSB. "Benediction of the Blessed Sacrament." In *New Catholic Encyclopedia.* Vol. 2, pp. 303–4. Washington, DC: Catholic University of America, 1967.

Burke, Kenneth. *The Philosophy of Literary Form*. 3rd ed. Berkeley: University of California Press, 1973.

Carpenter, Humphrey, ed. *Letters of J. R. R. Tolkien*. Boston: Houghton Mifflin, 1981.

Chapman, John, OSB. Review: Anscar Vonier, OSB, *A Key to the Doctrine of the Eucharist*. Westminster, MD: Newman Press, 1951. *Downside Review* 44 (1926): 95–98.

Corbon, Jean, OP. *The Wellspring of Worship*. New York-Mahwah, NJ: Paulist Press, 1988.

Countryman, L. William. *Forgiven and Forgiving*. Harrisburg: Morehouse, 1998.

———. *The Poetic Imagination: An Anglican Spiritual Tradition*. Maryknoll, NY: Orbis, 1999.

Crowley, Paul G., SJ. *Unwanted Wisdom: Suffering, the Cross and Hope*. New York: Continuum, 2005.

Cummings, Owen F. *Canterbury Cousins: Contemporary Anglican Eucharistic Theology*. New York / Mahwah, NJ: Paulist Press, 2007.

———. *Eucharistic Doctors*. New York / Mahwah, NJ: Paulist Press, 2005.

———. "James Dunlop Crichton (1907–2001)." *Antiphon* 6 (2001): 8–11.

———. *John Macquarrie: A Master of Theology*. New York / Mahwah, NJ: Paulist Press, 2002.

———. *The Theology of John Macquarrie: A Comprehensive and Contextual Exploration*. Lewiston, NY: Edwin Mellen, 2010.

———. *Thinking about Prayer*. Eugene, OR: Wipf and Stock, 2009.

Daly, Cathal. "Eucharistic Devotion." In *Understanding the Eucharist*, edited by Patrick McGoldrick. Dublin: Gill and Macmillan, 1969.

Driscoll, Jeremy, OSB. "Adoration of the Blessed Sacrament." In *A Book of Readings on the Eucharist*, pp. 85–92. Washington, DC: National Conference of Catholic Bishops, 2000.

———. *What Happens at Mass*. Chicago: Liturgy Training Publications, 2005.

Duffy, Regis A., OFM. "Reconciliation." In *The New Dictionary of Theology,* edited by J. A. Komonchak, M. Collins, and D. A. Lane, pp. 830–36. Collegeville, MN: Liturgical Press, 1987.

Evans, Gillian Red. "Alan of Lille." In *Concise Encyclopedia of Preaching,* edited by William H. Willimon and Richard Lischer, pp. 9–10. Louisville: Westminster John Knox Press, 1995.

——. *Alan of Lille: The Art of Preaching.* Kalamazoo, MI: Cistercian Publications, 1981.

——. *Alan of Lille: The Frontiers of Theology in the Later Twelfth Century.* Cambridge, UK: Cambridge University Press, 1983.

——. *Philosophy and Theology in the Middle Ages.* London: Routledge, 1993.

Favazza, Joseph A. "The Eucharistic Table, a Reconciling Table? Our Belief, Our Experience, Our Dilemma." In *The Many Presences of Christ,* edited by Timothy Fitzgerald and David A. Lysik, pp. 82–96. Chicago: Liturgy Training Publications, 1999.

Ford, David F. *The Future of Christian Theology.* Oxford and Chichester, UK: Blackwell-Wiley, 2011.

——. "George Herbert: The Centrality of God." *Theology* 96 (1993): 357–64.

——. *The Shape of Living.* London: HarperCollins, 1997.

Gallagher, Michael Paul, SJ. "Praying: Ringing in the Changes." *Furrow* 39 (1988): 689–95.

Gilbert, Sandra M., ed. *Inventions of Farewell: A Book of Elegies* (New York and London: Norton, 2001).

Glorieux, P. "Alan of Lille." In *New Catholic Encyclopedia.* Vol. 1, pp. 239–40. Washington, DC: Catholic University of America, 1967.

Gomes, Peter. "Preaching as a Matter of Trust: Recovering the Nerve of the Pulpit." In *Theology in the Service of the Church,* edited by Wallace M. Alston Jr., pp. 100–116. Grand Rapids: Eerdmans, 2000.

Graf, Ernest, OSB. "Abbot Anscar Vonier." *In Memoriam Abbot Vonier,* pp. 22–30. Buckfast, UK: Buckfast Abbey Chronicle, 1939.

——. *Abbot Vonier.* Westminster, MD: Newman Press, 1957.

Greeley, Andrew M. *The Catholic Imagination.* Berkeley-Los Angeles-London: University of California Press, 2000.

Hauerwas, Stanley. *Dispatches from the Front.* Durham and London: Duke University Press, 1994.

Holmes, Peter. *Adversus Praxean.* In *The Writings of Tertullian.* Vol. II. Edinburgh: T. and T. Clark, 1870.

Irwin, Kevin W. "Authentic Worship in Spirit and in Truth." *Pastoral Music* (October 2008): 51.

James, William. *The Varieties of Religious Experience.* London: Longmans Green, 1941.

Jasper, Ronald C. D., and Geoffrey J. Cuming, eds. *Prayers of the Eucharist: Early and Reformed.* 3rd ed. New York: Pueblo, 1987.

Jones, L. Gregory. "The Craft of Forgiveness." *Theology Today* 50 (1993): 345–57.

———. *Embodying Forgiveness: A Theological Analysis.* Grand Rapids: Eerdmans, 1995.

Kasper, Walter. *The God of Jesus Christ.* London: SCM, 1983.

Kavanagh, Aidan, OSB. *On Liturgical Theology.* New York: Pueblo, 1984.

Kennedy, V. L., CSB. "The Moment of Consecration and the Elevation of the Host." *Medieval Studies* 6 (1944): 121–50.

Kerr, Fergus, OP. *Theology after Wittgenstein.* Oxford, UK: Blackwell, 1986.

Kilmartin, Edward J., SJ. *The Eucharist in the West: History and Theology.* Collegeville, MN: Liturgical Press, 1998.

LaCugna, Catherine. "Trinity and Liturgy." In *The New Dictionary of Sacramental Worship,* edited by Peter E. Fink, SJ, pp. 1294–96. Collegeville, MN: Liturgical Press, 1990.

Laurance, John D., SJ. "The Eucharist and Eucharistic Adoration." *Louvain Studies* 26 (2001): 313–33.

Louth, Andrew. *Discerning the Mystery.* Oxford, UK: Clarendon Press, 1983.

Mackey, James P. *Jesus the Man and the Myth.* New York / Ramsey, NJ: Paulist Press, 1979.

John Macquarrie. *A Guide to the Sacraments.* New York: Continuum, 1997.

———. *Paths in Spirituality.* 2nd ed. Harrisburg: Morehouse, 1992.

Mannion, M. Francis. *Masterworks of God: Essays in Liturgical Theory and Practice.* Chicago/Mundelein: Hillenbrand Books/Liturgy Training Publications, 2004.

Martini, Carlo M., SJ. "The School of the Word." *Worship* 61 (1987): 194–98.

Mascall, Eric L. *Corpus Christi.* London-New York-Toronto: Longmans, Green and Co., 1953.

Mazza, Enrico. *The Eucharistic Prayers of the Roman Rite.* New York: Pueblo, 1986.

McIntosh, Mark. *Mystical Theology.* Oxford, UK: Blackwell, 1998.

McNeil, Brian, CRV. *The Master Is Here: Biblical Reflections on Eucharistic Adoration.* Dublin: Veritas, 1997.

McPartlan, Paul. "Go Forth, Christian Soul." *One in Christ* 34 (1998): 247–57.

Michaels, Anne. *Fugitive Pieces.* London: Bloomsbury, 1998.

Mitchell, Nathan, OSB. *Cult and Controversy: The Worship of the Eucharist outside Mass.* New York: Pueblo, 1982.

Moloney, Raymond, SJ. "The Doctrine of the Eucharist." In *Commentary on the Catechism of the Catholic Church,* edited by Michael J. Walsh, pp. 259–73. Collegeville, MN: Liturgical Press, 1994.

———. *The Eucharist.* Collegeville, MN: Liturgical Press, 1995.

———. *The Eucharistic Prayers in Worship, Preaching and Study.* Dublin: Dominican Publications, 1985.

———. *Our Splendid Eucharist.* Dublin: Veritas, 2003.

Neuner, Joseph, and Jacques Dupuis, eds. *The Christian Faith in the Doctrinal Documents of the Catholic Church.* Rev. ed. London: Collins, 1983.

Nichols, Aidan, OP. *Dominican Gallery: Portrait of a Culture.* Leominster, UK: Fowler Wright, 1997.

———. *The Holy Eucharist.* Dublin: Veritas, 1991.

———. *The Service of Glory.* Edinburgh: T. and T. Clark, 1997.

O'Donoghue, Noel Dermot, ODC. *The Holy Mountain: Approaches to the Mystery of Prayer*. Wilmington, DE: Michael Glazier, 1983.

O'Donohue, John. *Anam Chara*. New York: HarperCollins, 1997.

O'Faolain, Nuala. *My Dream of You*. New York: Riverhead, 2001.

O'Neill, Colman, OP. *Sacramental Realism*. Wilmington, DE: Michael Glazier, 1983.

Pattison, George. *The End of Theology and the Task of Thinking about God*. London: SCM, 1998.

Phillips, Dewi Z. *The Concept of Prayer*. New York: Seabury, 1981.

Preston, Geoffrey, OP. *Faces of the Church*. Edinburgh: T. and T. Clark, 1997.

———. *Hallowing the Time*. New York / Ramsey, NJ: Paulist Press, 1980.

Quick, Oliver C. *The Christian Sacraments*. London: Nisbet, 1927.

Radcliffe, Timothy, OP. *I Call You Friends*. New York and London: Continuum, 2001.

———. *Sing a New Song: The Christian Vocation*. Springfield, IL: Templegate, 1999.

Rahner, Karl, SJ. "The Eucharist and Suffering." In *Theological Investigations*. Vol. 3, pp. 161–70. New York: Seabury, 1974.

———. "Eucharistic Worship." In *Theological Investigations*. Vol. 23, pp. 113–16. New York: Crossroad, 1992.

Ratzinger, Joseph / Pope Benedict XVI. *Jesus of Nazareth, Part Two: Holy Week*. San Francisco: Ignatius Press, 2011.

Rawlins, Clive L. *William Barclay: The Authorized Biography*. Grand Rapids: Eerdmans, 1984.

Raymo, Chet. *Climbing Brandon: Science and Faith on Ireland's Holy Mountain*. New York: Walker and Co., 2004.

Richards, Hubert J. *What Happens When You Pray?* London: SCM, 1980.

Schmemann, Alexander. *The Eucharist*. Crestwood, NY: St. Vladimir's Seminary Press, 1988.

Searle, Mark. "Benediction." In *Encyclopedia of Catholicism*, edited by Richard P. McBrien, p. 155. San Francisco: HarperCollins, 1995.

Slater, Ann P., ed. *George Herbert: The Complete English Works*. London: David Campbell, 1995.

Smart, Ninian. *The Religious Experience of Mankind*. New York: Scribner's, 1969.

Sokolowski, Robert. "Steps into the Eucharist: the Phenomenology of the Mass." *Crisis* 12 (September 1994): 16–21.

Spufford, Margaret. *Celebration: A Story of Suffering and Joy*. London: Mowbray, 1989.

Strier, Richard. *Love Known: Theology and Experience in George Herbert's Poetry*. Chicago and London: University of Chicago Press, 1983.

Suchocki, Marjorie. *God-Christ-Church*. Rev. ed. New York: Crossroad, 1989.

———. *In God's Presence: Theological Reflections on Prayer*. St. Louis, MO: Chalice, 1996.

Surin, Kenneth. *Theology and the Problem of Evil*. Oxford, UK: Blackwell, 1986.

Tanner, Norman P., SJ, ed. *Decrees of the Ecumenical Councils*. Vols. I–II. London and Washington, DC: Sheed & Ward and Georgetown University Press, 1990.

Thiel, John. *God, Evil and Innocent Suffering*. New York: Crossroad, 2000.

Thurian, Max. "The Liturgy and Contemplation." *Antiphon* 1 (1996): 2–6.

Tilley, Terrence W. *Evils of Theodicy*. Washington, DC: Georgetown University Press, 1991.

Tristram, Henry, ed. *John Henry Newman: Autobiographical Writings*. New York: Sheed and Ward, 1957.

Tutu, Desmond. *No Future without Forgiveness*. London: Rider, 1999.

Tyler, Anne. *Saint Maybe*. New York: Knopf, 1991.

Upson, Wilfred, OSB. "Abbot Anscar Vonier." *In Memoriam Abbot Vonier*, pp. 1–7. Buckfast, UK: Buckfast Abbey Chronicle, 1939.

Vatican II. Constitution on the Sacred Liturgy (*Sacrosanctum Concilium*), no. 7, accessible at http://www.vatican.va/archive/hist_councils/ii_vatican_council/documents/vat-ii_const_19631204_sacrosanctum-concilium_en.html.

Vatican II. Constitution on Divine Revelation (*Dei Verbum*), no. 21, accessible at http://www.vatican.va/archive/hist_councils/ii_vatican_council/documents/vat-ii_const_19651118_dei-verbum_en.html.

Visser, Margaret. *The Geometry of Love*. New York: North Point, 2000.

Vonier, Anscar, OSB. *A Key to the Doctrine of the Eucharist*. Westminster, MD: Newman Press, 1951.

Wainwright, Geoffrey. "The Ecumenical Rediscovery of the Trinity." *One in Christ* 34 (1998): 95–124.

———. *Worship with One Accord: Where Liturgy and Ecumenism Embrace*. New York and Oxford, UK: Oxford University Press, 1997, pp. 237–50.

Walsh, Liam, OP. *The Sacraments of Initiation*. London: Geoffrey Chapman, 1988.

Whelan, Joseph P., SJ. *Benjamin: Essays in Prayer*. New York-Paramus-Toronto: Newman Press, 1972.

Williams, Rowan D. *Open to Judgment: Sermons and Addresses*. London: Darton, Longman and Todd, 1994.

———. "The Sermon." In *Living the Eucharist*, edited by Stephen Conway, pp. 44–55. London: Darton, Longman and Todd, 2001.

Winterton, Gregory, ed. *The Dream of Gerontius*. London and Oxford: Mowbray, 1986.

Wright, John H., SJ. *A Theology of Christian Prayer*. New York: Pueblo, 1979.

Young, Frances M. *Face to Face*. London: Epworth, 1986.

———. "Suffering." In *The Oxford Companion to Christian Thought*, edited by Adrian Hastings et al., pp. 687–89. New York and Oxford, UK: Oxford University Press, 2000.